DATE OF RETURN
UNLESS RECALLED BY LIBRARY

PLEASE TAKE GOOD CARE OF THIS BOOK

THOMAS HOBBES   **MICHAEL OAKESHOTT**

Hobbes on
Civil Association

Michael Oakeshott

FOREWORD BY PAUL FRANCO

Liberty Fund

INDIANAPOLIS

© 1937, 1975 Liberty Fund, Inc.

Frontispiece of Michael Oakeshott courtesy Estate of Angus McBean.
Frontispiece of Thomas Hobbes courtesy of Corbis Bettman.

04 03 02 01 00 C 5 4 3 2 1
04 03 02 01 00 P 5 4 3 2 1

Library of Congress Cataloging-in-Publication Data

Oakeshott, Michael Joseph, 1901–
Hobbes on civil association/Michael Oakeshott;
foreword by Paul Franco.
p.   cm.
Includes bibliographical references.
ISBN 0-86597-290-7 (hc: alk. paper)
ISBN 0-86597-291-5 (pbk.: alk. paper)
1. Hobbes, Thomas, 1588–1679—Contributions in political science.
2. Civil society. I. Title.

JC153.H66 2000
320'.01—dc21   00-035410

Liberty Fund, Inc.
8335 Allison Pointe Trail, Suite 300
Indianapolis, Indiana 46250-1684

Contents

Foreword

Though Michael Oakeshott (1901–1990) is best known as a political philosopher in his own right, he was also a profound student of the history of political philosophy, and he was a major scholar on the thought of Thomas Hobbes. Oakeshott's interest in Hobbes emerged quite early in his career—he wrote a review-essay of recent Hobbes scholarship in 1935[1]—and it continued throughout most of his life—he published a lengthy review of a book on Hobbes in 1974.[2] It seems at first strange that this last gasp of the British idealist school—in his first book, *Experience and Its Modes* (1933), Oakeshott named Hegel and F. H. Bradley as his greatest influences—should have turned to Hobbes for inspiration, but the development of Oakeshott's political philosophy gradually revealed the deep affinities he had with his seventeenth-century predecessor. The themes Oakeshott stresses in his interpretation of Hobbes are, for the most part, themes that animate his own political philosophy: skepticism about the role of reason in politics, allegiance to the morality of individuality as opposed to any sort of collectivism, and the idea of a noninstrumental, nonpurposive mode of political associa-

---

1. Michael Oakeshott, "Thomas Hobbes," *Scrutiny* 4 (1935–36), 263–77.

2. Michael Oakeshott, "Logos and Telos," *Government and Opposition* 9 (1971), 237–44; reprinted in *Rationalism in Politics and Other Essays* (Indianapolis: Liberty Fund, 1991), 351–59.

tion, namely, civil association. This last-named idea receives explicit recognition in the title Oakeshott chose for this volume.

With the exception of the reviews mentioned above, the essays collected in this volume (which was originally published in 1975) represent almost the whole of Oakeshott's writings on Hobbes. By the elephantine standards of contemporary scholarship, it may seem a rather slender output, but Oakeshott disdained the more industrial side of academic scholarship, and he generally packs more into a single essay than most authors manage to express in an entire book. It is indisputable that these essays—especially the Introduction to *Leviathan* and "The Moral Life in the Writings of Thomas Hobbes"—have influenced Hobbes studies far beyond their modest length and that they disclose a distinctive portrait of Hobbes with which any contemporary scholar of Hobbes's philosophy must come to terms.

The earliest of the essays is "Dr. Leo Strauss on Hobbes" (1937), an admiring but not uncritical review of Strauss's important book *The Political Philosophy of Hobbes: Its Basis and Its Genesis.* One of the things that no doubt attracted Oakeshott to this book (which he actually reviewed three different times)[3] was its attempt to replace the traditional, positivist image of Hobbes as a naturalistic philosopher engaged in a scientific analysis of politics with an image of Hobbes as a genuine moral philosopher. Though Oakeshott shares this general aspiration with Strauss, he rejects Strauss's specific argument that the original and real basis of Hobbes's political philosophy was a prescientific moral attitude upon which Hobbes in his mature writings merely superimposed a scientific form but never really abandoned. For Oakeshott, the argument of *Leviathan* constitutes a genuine advance in Hobbes's philosophical thinking, not because it is more "scientific"—to Oakeshott "Hobbes was never a scientist in any true sense . . . his 'science' is conceived throughout as an episte-

---

3. Besides the review contained in this volume, he reviewed Strauss's book in *The Cambridge Review* 57 (1936–37), 150; and in *Philosophy* 12 (1937), 239–41.

Introduction to *Leviathan*

"We are discussing no trivial subject, but how a man should live."
—Plato, *Republic*, 352D.

I. Biographical

Thomas Hobbes, the second son of an otherwise undistinguished vicar of Westport, near Malmesbury, was born in the spring of 1588. He was educated at Malmesbury where he became an exceptional scholar in Latin and Greek, and at Oxford where in the course of five years he maintained his interest in classical literature and became acquainted with the theological controversies of the day, but was taught only some elementary logic and Aristotelian physics.

In 1608 he was appointed tutor (and later became secretary) to the son of William Cavendish, first Earl of Devonshire. For the whole of his adult life Hobbes maintained a close relationship with the Cavendish family, passing many of his years as a member of the household either at Chatsworth or in London. In these circumstances he came to meet some of the leading politicians and literary men of his day, Bacon and Jonson among them. The year 1610 he spent in France and Italy with his charge, getting a first glimpse of the intellectual life of the continent and returning with a determination to make himself a scholar. The next eighteen years, passed mostly at Chatsworth, were the germinating period of his future intellectual interests and activities. There is little record of how precisely they were spent, and the only literary product of this period of his life was the translation of Thucydides, published in 1629: but there can be no doubt that philosophy occupied his mind increasingly.

On the death of the second Earl of Devonshire in 1628, Hobbes accepted the position of tutor to the son of Sir Gervase Clinton, with whom he stayed three years, two of which were spent on the continent. It was at this time that Hobbes discovered for himself the intellectual world of mathematics and geometry, a world so important to the continental philosophers of his time, but of which hitherto he had been entirely ignorant. The discovery gave renewed impetus and fresh direction to his philosophical reflections, and from then philosophy dominated his mind.

In 1631 Hobbes returned to the Cavendish household as tutor to the new earl, with whom he made his third visit to the continent (1634–37). It was on this visit that he met Galileo in Florence and became acquainted with the circle of philosophers centred round Mersenne in Paris, and particularly with Gassendi. And on his return to England he completed in 1640 (but did not publish until 1650) his first important piece of philosophical writing, the *Elements of Law*. He was fifty-two years old, and he had in his head the plan of a philosophy which he desired to expound systematically.

The next eleven years were spent in Paris, free for a while from extraneous duties. But instead of embarking at once on the composition of the most general part of his philosophy—his philosophy of nature—he wrote *De Cive*, an exposition of his political philosophy, which was published in 1642. Paris for Hobbes was a society for philosophers; but in 1645 it became the home of the exiled court of Charles, Prince of Wales, and Hobbes was appointed tutor to the prince. His mind still ran on the philosophy of politics, and in 1651 his masterpiece, *Leviathan*, was published.

In 1652 he returned to England, took up his place (which he was never again to leave) in the household of the Earl of Devonshire, and set about the composition of the rest of his philosophical system. In 1655 was published *De Corpore*, and in 1658 *De Homine*. He had still twenty years to live. They were years of incessant literary activity and of philosophical, mathematical, theological, and political controversy. After the Restoration he was received at Court, and he spent much of his time in London. In 1675, however, perceiving that he must soon retire from the world, he retired to Chatsworth. He died in the winter of 1679 at the age of ninety-one.

II. The Context of *Leviathan*

Leviathan is the greatest, perhaps the sole, masterpiece of political philosophy written in the English language. And the history of our civilization can provide only a few works of similar scope and achievement to set beside it. Consequently, it must be judged by none but the highest standards and must be considered only in the widest context. The masterpiece supplies a standard and a context for the second-rate, which indeed is but a gloss; but the context of the masterpiece itself, the setting in which its meaning is revealed, can in the nature of things be nothing narrower than the history of political philosophy.

Reflection about political life may take place at a variety of levels. It may remain on the level of the determination of means, or it may strike out for the consideration of ends. Its inspiration may be directly practical, the modification of the arrangements of a political order in accordance with the perception of an immediate benefit; or it may be practical, but less directly so, guided by general ideas. Or again, springing from an experience of political life, it may seek a generalization of that experience in a doctrine. And reflection is apt to flow from one level to another in an unbroken movement, following the mood of the thinker. Political philosophy may be understood to be what occurs when this movement of reflection takes a certain direction and achieves a certain level, its characteristic being the relation of political life, and the values and purposes pertaining to it, to the entire conception of the world that belongs to a civilization. That is to say, at all other levels of reflection on political life we have before us the single world of political activity, and what we are interested in is the internal coherence of that world; but in political philosophy we have in our minds that world and another world, and our endeavour is to explore the coherence of the two worlds together. The reflective intelligence is apt to find itself at this level without the consciousness of any great conversion and without any sense of entering upon a new project, but merely by submitting itself to the impetus of reflection, by spreading its sails to the argument. For any man who holds in his mind the conceptions of the natural world, of God, of human activity and human destiny which belong to his civilization will scarcely be able to prevent an endeavour to assimilate these to the ideas that distinguish the political order in which he lives, and failing to do so he will become a philosopher (of a simple sort) unawares.

But, though we may stumble over the frontier of philosophy unwittingly and by doing nothing more demonstrative than refusing to draw rein, to achieve significant reflection, of course, requires more than inadvertence and more than the mere acceptance of the two worlds of ideas. The whole impetus of the enterprise is the perception that what really exists is a single world of ideas, which comes to us divided by the abstracting force of circumstances; is the perception that our political ideas and what may be called the rest of our ideas are not in fact two independent worlds, and that though they may come to us as separate text and context, the *meaning* lies, as it always must lie, in a unity in which the separate existence of text and context is resolved.

We may begin, probably we must begin, with an independent valuation of the text and the context; but the impetus of reflection is not spent until we have restored in detail the unity of which we had a prevision. And, so far, philosophical reflection about politics will be nothing other than the intellectual restoration of a unity damaged and impaired by the normal negligence of human partiality. But to have gone so far is already to have raised questions the answers to which are not to be found in any fresh study of what is behind us. Even if we accept the standards and valuations of our civilization, it will be only by putting an arbitrary closure on reflection that we can prevent the consideration of the meaning of the general terms in which those standards are expressed; good and evil, right and wrong, justice and injustice. And, turning, we shall catch sight of all that we have learned reflected in the *speculum universitatis.*

Now, whether or not this can be defended as a hypothetical conception of the nature of political philosophy, it certainly describes a form of reflection about politics that has a continuous history in our civilization. To establish the connections, in principle and in detail, directly or mediately, between politics and eternity is a project that has never been without its followers. Indeed, the pursuit of this project is only a special arrangement of the whole intellectual life of our civilization; it is the whole intellectual history organized and exhibited from a particular angle of vision. Probably there has been no theory of the nature of the world, of the activity of man, of the destiny of mankind, no theology or cosmology, perhaps even no metaphysics, that has not sought a reflection of itself in the mirror of political philosophy; certainly there has been no fully considered politics that has not looked for its reflection in eternity. This history of political philosophy is, then, the context of the masterpiece. And to interpret it in the context of this history secures it against the deadening requirement of conformity to a merely abstract idea of political philosophy.

This kind of reflection about politics is not, then, to be denied a place in our intellectual history. And it is characteristic of political philosophers that they take a sombre view of the human situation: they deal in darkness. Human life in their writings appears, generally, not as a feast or even as a journey, but as a predicament; and the link between politics and eternity is the contribution the political order is conceived as making to the deliverance of mankind. Even those whose thought is most remote from violent contrasts of dark and light (Aristotle, for example) do not altogether avoid this disposition of mind. And some political philosophers may even be suspected of spreading darkness in order to make their light more acceptable. Man, so the varied formula runs, is the dupe of error, the slave of sin, of passion, of fear, of care, the enemy of himself or of others or of both—

O miseras hominum mentes, O pectora caeca

—and the civil order appears as the whole or a part of the scheme of his salvation. The precise manner in which the predicament is conceived, the qualities of mind and imagination and the kinds of activity man can bring to the achievement of his own salvation, the exact nature and power of civil arrangements and institutions, the urgency, the method and the comprehensiveness of the deliverance—these are the singularities of each political philosophy. In them are reflected the intellectual achievements of the epoch or society, and the great and slowly mediated changes in intellectual habit and horizon that have overtaken our civilization. Every masterpiece of political philosophy springs from a new vision of the predicament; each is the glimpse of a deliverance or the suggestion of a remedy.

It will not, then, surprise us to find an apparently contingent element in the ground and inspiration of a political philosophy, a feeling for the exigencies, the cares, the passions of a particular time, a sensitiveness to the dominant folly of an epoch: for the human predicament is a universal appearing everywhere as a particular. Plato's thought is animated by the errors of Athenian democracy, Augustine's by the sack of Rome, and what stirs the mind of Hobbes is "grief for the present calamities of my country," a country torn between those who claimed too much for Liberty and those who claimed too much for Authority, a country given over into the hands of ambitious men who enlisted the envy and resentment of a "giddy people" for the advancement of their ambitions.[1, 2] And not being surprised at this element of particularity, we shall not allow it to mislead us into supposing that nothing more is required to make a political philosopher than an impressionable political consciousness; for the masterpiece, at least, is always the revelation of the universal predicament in the local and transitory mischief.[3]

If the unity of the history of political philosophy lies in a pervading sense of human life as a predicament and in the continuous reflection of the changing climate of the European intellectual scene, its significant variety will be found in three great traditions of thought. The singularities of political philosophies (like most singularities) are not unique, but follow one of three main patterns which philosophical reflection about politics has impressed upon the intellectual history of Europe. These I call traditions because it belongs to the nature of a tradition to tolerate and unite an internal variety, not insisting upon conformity to a single character, and because, further, it has the ability to change without losing its identity. The first of these traditions is distinguished by the master-conceptions of Reason and Nature. It is coeval with our civilization; it has an unbroken history into the modern world; and it has survived by a matchless power of adaptability all the changes of the European consciousness. The

1. *E.W.*, II, i–xxiv.
2. *L.*, pp. 3, 274, 549. Hobbes had also in mind the situation in late sixteenth-century France.
3. *L.*, p. 271.

master-conceptions of the second are Will and Artifice. It too springs from the soil of Greece, and has drawn inspiration from many sources, not least from Israel and Islam. The third tradition is of later birth, not appearing until the eighteenth century. The cosmology it reflects in its still unsettled surface is the world seen on the analogy of human history. Its master-conception is the Rational Will, and its followers may be excused the belief that in it the truths of the first two traditions are fulfilled and their errors find a happy release. The masterpiece of political philosophy has for its context, not only the history of political philosophy as the elucidation of the predicament and deliverance of mankind, but also, normally, a particular tradition in that history; generally speaking it is the supreme expression of its own tradition. And, as Plato's *Republic* might be chosen as the representative of the first tradition, and Hegel's *Philosophie des Rechts* of the third, so *Leviathan* is the head and crown of the second.

Leviathan is a masterpiece, and we must understand it according to our means. If our poverty is great, but not ruinous, we may read it not looking beyond its two covers, but intend to draw from it nothing that is not there. This will be a notable achievement, if somewhat narrow. The reward will be the appreciation of a dialectical triumph with all the internal movement and liveliness of such a triumph. But *Leviathan* is more than a *tour de force*. And something of its larger character will be perceived if we read it with the other works of Hobbes open beside it. Or again, at greater expense of learning, we may consider it in its tradition, and doing so will find fresh meaning in the world of ideas it opens to us. But finally, we may discover in it the true character of a masterpiece—the still centre of a whirlpool of ideas which has drawn into itself numberless currents of thought, contemporary and historic, and by its centripetal force has shaped and compressed them into a momentary significance before they are flung off again into the future.

III. The Mind and Manner

In the mind of a man, the σύνολον of form and content alone is actual; style and matter, method and doctrine, are inseparable. And when the mind is that of a philosopher, it is a sound rule to come to consider the technical expression of this unity only after it has been observed in the less formal version of it that appears in temperament, cast of mind, and style of writing. Circumstantial evidence of this sort can, of course, contribute nothing relevant to the substantiation of the technical distinctions of a philosophy; but often it has something to contribute to the understanding of them. At least, I think this is so with Hobbes.

Philosophy springs from a certain bent of mind which, though different in character, is as much a natural gift as an aptitude for mathematics or a genius for music. Philosophical speculation requires so little in the way of a knowledge of the world and is, in comparison with some other intellectual pursuits, so independent of book-learning, that the gift is apt to manifest itself early in life. And often a philosopher will be found to have made his significant contribution at an age when others are still preparing themselves to speak or to act. Hobbes had a full share of the *anima naturaliter philosophica,* yet it is remarkable that the beginning of his philosophical writing cannot be dated before his forty-second year and that his masterpiece was written when he was past sixty. Certainly there is nothing precocious in his genius; but are we to suppose that the love of reasoning, the passion for dialectic, which belong to the gift for philosophy, were absent from his character in youth? Writers on Hobbes have been apt to take a short way with this suggestion of a riddle. The life of Hobbes has been divided into neat periods, and his appearance as a philosopher in middle life has been applauded rather than explained. Brilliant at school, idle at the university, unambitious in early life, later touched by a feeling for scholarship and finally taking the path of philosophy when, at the age of forty, the power

of geometric proof was revealed to him in the pages of *Euclid:*
such is the life attributed to him. It leaves something to be desired. And evidence has been collected which goes to show that
philosophy and geometry were not coeval in Hobbes's mind, evidence that the speculative gift was not unexercised in his earlier
years.[4] Yet it remains true that when he appears as a philosophical writer, he is already adult, mature in mind; the period of eager search of tentative exploration, goes unreflected in his pages.

   The power and confidence of Hobbes's mind as he comes before us in his writings cannot escape observation. He is arrogant
(but it is not the arrogance of youth), dogmatic, and when he
speaks it is in a tone of confident finality: he knows everything
except how his doctrines will be received. There is nothing
half-formed or undeveloped in him, nothing in progress; there is
no promise, only fulfilment. There is self-confidence, also, a
Montaigne-like self-confidence; he has accepted himself and he
expects others to accept him on the same terms. And all this is
understandable when we appreciate that Hobbes is not one of
those philosophers who allow us to see the workings of their
minds, and that he published nothing until he was fifty-four
years old. There are other, more technical, reasons for his confidence. His conception of philosophy as the establishment by
reasoning of hypothetical causes saved him from the necessity of
observing the caution appropriate to those who deal with facts
and events.[5] But, at bottom, it springs from his maturity, the
knowledge that before he spoke he was a match for anyone who
had the temerity to answer back. It belonged to Hobbes's temperament and his art, not less than to his circumstances, to hold
his fire. His long life after middle age gave him the room for
change and development that others find in earlier years; but he
did not greatly avail himself of it. He was often wrong, especially
in his light-hearted excursions into mathematics, and he often

   4. L. Strauss, *The Political Philosophy of Hobbes.*
   5. *L.*, p. 554.

changed his views, but he rarely retracted an opinion. His confidence never deserted him.

But if the first impression of Hobbes's philosophical writing is one of maturity and deliberateness, the second is an impression of remarkable energy. It is as if all the lost youth of Hobbes's mind had been recovered and perpetuated in this preeminently youthful quality. One of the more revealing observations of Aubrey about him is that "he was never idle; his thoughts were always working." And from this energy flow the other striking characteristics of his mind and manner—his scepticism, his addiction to system, and his passion for controversy.

An impulse for philosophy may originate in faith (as with Erigena), or in curiosity (as with Locke), but with Hobbes the prime mover was doubt. Scepticism was, of course, in the air he breathed; but in an age of sceptics he was the most radical of them all. His was not the elegiac scepticism of Montaigne, nor the brittle net in which Pascal struggled, nor was it the methodological doubt of Descartes; for him it was both a method and a conclusion, purging and creative. It is not the technicalities of his scepticism (which we must consider later) that are so remarkable, but its ferocity. A medieval passion overcomes him as he sweeps aside into a common abyss of absurdity both the believer in eternal truth and the industrious seeker after truths; both faith and science. Indeed, so extravagant, so heedless of consequences, is his scepticism, that the reader is inclined to exclaim, what Hobbes himself is said to have exclaimed on seeing the proof of the forty-seventh theorem in *Euclid,* "By God, this is impossible." And what alone makes his scepticism plausible is the intrepidity of Hobbes himself; he has the nerve to accept his conclusions and the confidence to build on them. Both the energy to destroy and the energy to construct are powerful in Hobbes.

A man, it is generally agreed, may make himself ridiculous as easily by a philosophical system as by any other means. And yet, the impulse to think systematically is, at bottom, nothing more

than the conscientious pursuit of what is for every philosopher
the end to be achieved. The passion for clearness and simplicity,
the determination not to be satisfied with anything inconse-
quent, the refusal to relieve one element of experience at the
cost of another, are the motives of all philosophical thinking;
and they conduce to system. "The desire of wisdom leadeth to
a kingdom." And the pursuit of system is a call, not only upon
fine intelligence and imagination, but also, and perhaps preeminently, upon energy of mind. For the principle in system is not
the simple exclusion of all that does not fit, but the perpetual
reestablishment of coherence. Hobbes stands out, not only
among his contemporaries, but also in the history of English philosophy, as the creator of a system. And he conceived this system
with such imaginative power that, in spite of its relatively simple
character, it bears comparison with even the grand and subtle
creation of Hegel. But if it requires great energy of mind to create a system, it requires even greater not to become the slave of
the creation. To become the slave of a system in life is not to
know when to "hang up philosophy," not to recognize the final
triumph of inconsequence; in philosophy, it is not to know when
the claims of comprehension outweigh those of coherence. And
here also the energy of Hobbes's mind did not desert him. When
we come to consider the technicalities of his philosophy we shall
observe a moderation that, for example, allowed him to escape
an atomic philosophy, and an absence of rigidity that allowed
him to modify his philosophical method when dealing with politics; here, when we are considering informally the quality of his
mind, this ability appears as resilience, the energy to be perpetually freeing himself from the formalism of his system.

Thinking, for Hobbes, was not only conceived as movement,
it was felt as movement. Mind is something agile, thoughts are
darting, and the language of passion is appropriate to describe
their workings. And the energy of his nature made it impossible
for him not to take pleasure in controversy. The blood of contention ran in his veins. He acquired the lucid genius of a great

expositor of ideas; but by disposition he was a fighter, and he knew no tactics save attack. He was a brilliant controversialist, deft, pertinacious and imaginative, and he disposed of the errors of scholastics, Puritans, and Papists with a subtle mixture of argument and ridicule. But he made the mistake of supposing that this style was universally effective, in mathematics no less than in politics. For brilliance in controversy is a corrupting accomplishment. Always to play to win is to take one's standards from one's opponent, and local victory comes to displace every other consideration. Most readers will find Hobbes's disputatiousness excessive; but it is the defect of an exceptionally active mind. And it never quite destroyed in him the distinction between beating an opponent and establishing a proposition, and never quite silenced the conversation with himself which is the heart of philosophical thinking. But, like many controversialists, he hated error more than he loved truth, and came to depend overmuch on the stimulus of opposition. There is sagacity in Hobbes, and often a profound deliberateness; but there is no repose.

We have found Hobbes to possess remarkable confidence and energy of mind; we must consider now whether his mind was also original. Like Epicurus, he had an affectation for originality. He rarely mentions a writer to acknowledge a debt, and often seems oversensitive about his independence of the past in philosophy. Aristotle's philosophy is "vain," and scholasticism is no more than a "collection of absurdities." But, though he had certainly read more than he sometimes cared to admit—it was a favourite saying of his that if he had read as much as other men he should have known no more than other men—he seems to have been content with the reading that happened to come his way, and complained rather of the inconvenience of a want of conversation at some periods in his life than of a lack of books. He was conscious of being a self-taught philosopher, an amateur, without the training of a Descartes or the background of a Spinoza. And this feeling was perhaps strengthened by the absence of an academic environment. One age of academic philosophy had gone, the next was yet to come. The seventeenth century was the age of the independent scholar, and Hobbes was one of these, taking his own way and making his own contacts with the learned world. And his profound suspicion of anything like authority in philosophy reinforced his circumstantial independence. The guidance he wanted he got from his touch with his contemporaries, particularly in Paris; his inspiration was a native sensitiveness to the direction required of philosophy if it were to provide an answer to the questions suggested by contemporary science. In conception and design, his philosophy is his own. And when he claimed that civil philosophy was "no older than my own book *De Cive*,"[6] he was expressing at once the personal achievement of having gone afresh to the facts of human consciousness for his interpretation of the meaning of civil association, and also that universal sense of newness with which his age appreciated its own intellectual accomplishments. But, for all that, his philosophy belongs to a tradition. Perhaps the truth is that Hobbes was as original as he thought he was, and to acknowledge his real indebtedness he would have required to see (what he could not be expected to see) the link between scholasticism and modern philosophy which is only now becoming clear to us. His philosophy is in the nature of a palimpsest. For its author what was important was what he wrote, and it is only to be expected that he should be indifferent to what is already there; but for us both sets of writing are significant.

Finally, Hobbes is a *writer*, a self-conscious stylist and the master of an individual style that expresses his whole personality; for there is no hiatus between his personality and his philosophy. His manner of writing is not, of course, foreign to his age; it belongs to him neither to write with the informality that is the achievement of Locke, nor with the simplicity that makes Hume's style a model not to be rejected by the philosophical writer of today. Hobbes is elaborate in an age that delighted in elaboration. But, within the range of his opportunities, he found

6. *E.W.*, I, ix.

a way of writing that exactly reflected his temperament. His con-
troversial purpose is large on every page; he wrote to convince
and to refute. And that in itself is a discipline. He has eloquence,
the charm of wit, the decisiveness of confidence and the senten-
tiousness of a mind made up: he is capable of urbanity and of
savage irony. But the most significant qualities of his style are
its didactic and its imaginative character. Philosophy in general
knows two styles, the contemplative and the didactic, although
there are many writers to whom neither belongs to the complete
exclusion of the other. Those who practice the first let us into
the secret workings of their minds and are less careful to send
us away with a precisely formulated doctrine. Philosophy for
them is a conversation, and, whether or not they write it as a
dialogue, their style reflects their conception. Hobbes's way of
writing is an example of the second style. What he says is already
entirely freed from the doubts and hesitancies of the process of
thought. It is only a residue, a distillate that is offered to the
reader. The defect of such a style is that the reader must either
accept or reject; if it inspires to fresh thought, it does so only
by opposition. And Hobbes's style is imaginative, not merely on
account of the subtle imagery that fills his pages, nor only because it requires imagination to make a system. His imagination
appears also as the power to create a myth. *Leviathan* is a myth,
the transposition of an abstract argument into the world of the
imagination. In it we are made aware at a glance of the fixed and
simple centre of a universe of complex and changing relationships. The argument may not be the better for this transposition,
and what it gains in vividness it may pay for in illusion. But it is
an accomplishment of art that Hobbes, in the history of political
philosophy, shares only with Plato.

IV. The System

In Hobbes's mind, his "civil philosophy" belonged to a system of
philosophy. Consequently, an enquiry into the character of this

system is not to be avoided by the interpreter of his politics. For, if the details of the civil theory may not improperly be considered as elements in a coherence of their own, the significance of the theory as a whole must depend upon the system to which it belongs, and upon the place it occupies in the system.

Two views, it appears, between them hold the field at the present time. The first is the view that the foundation of Hobbes's philosophy is a doctrine of materialism, that the intention of his system was the progressive revelation of this doctrine in nature, in man, and in society, and that this revelation was achieved in his three most important philosophical works, *De Corpore, De Homine,* and *De Cive.* These works, it is suggested, constitute a continuous argument, part of which is reproduced in *Leviathan;* and the novel project of the "civil philosophy" was the exposition of a politics based upon a "natural philosophy," the assimilation of politics to a materialistic doctrine of the world, or (it is even suggested) to the view of the world as it appeared in the conclusions of the physical sciences. A mechanistic-materialist politics is made to spring from a mechanistic-materialist universe. And, not improperly, it is argued that the significance of what appears at the end is determined at least in part by what was proved or assumed at the beginning. The second view is that this, no doubt, was the intention of Hobbes, but that "the attempt and not the deed confounds him." The joints of the system are ill-matched, and what should have been a continuous argument, based upon a philosophy of materialism, collapses under its own weight.

Both these views are, I think, misconceived. But they are the product not merely of inattention to the words of Hobbes; it is to be feared that they derive also from a graver fault of interpretation, a false expectation with regard to the nature of a philosophical system. For what is expected here is that a philosophical system should conform to an architectural analogue, and consequently what is sought in Hobbes's system is a foundation and a superstructure planned as a single whole, with civil philosophy as the top storey. Now, it may be doubted whether any philosophical system can properly be represented in the terms of architecture, but what is certain is that the analogy does violence to the system of Hobbes. The coherence of his philosophy, the system of it, lies not in an architectonic structure, but in a single "passionate thought" that pervades its parts.[7] The system is not the plan or key of the labyrinth of the philosophy; it is, rather, a guiding clue, like the thread of Ariadne.[8] It is like the music that gives meaning to the movement of dancers, or the law of evidence that gives coherence to the practice of a court. And the thread, the hidden thought, is the continuous application of a doctrine about the nature of philosophy. Hobbes's philosophy is the world reflected in the mirror of the philosophic eye, each image the representation of a fresh object, but each determined by the character of the mirror itself. In short, the civil philosophy belongs to a philosophical system, not because it is materialistic but because it is philosophical; and an enquiry into the character of the system and the place of politics in it resolves itself into an enquiry into what Hobbes considered to be the nature of philosophy.

For Hobbes, to think philosophically is to reason; philosophy is reasoning. To this all else is subordinate; from this all else derives. It is the character of reasoning that determines the range and the limits of philosophical enquiry; it is this character that gives coherence, system, to Hobbes's philosophy. Philosophy, for him, is the world as it appears in the mirror of reason; civil philosophy is the image of the civil order reflected in that mirror. In general, the world seen in this mirror is a world of causes and effects: cause and effect are its categories. And for Hobbes reason has two alternative ends: to determine the conditional causes of given effects, or to determine the conditional effects of given

---

7. Confucius said, "T'zu, you probably think that I have learned many things and hold them in my mind." "Yes," he replied, "is that not true?" "No," said Confucius; "I have one thing that permeates everything."—Confucius, *Analects*, XV, 2. *L.*, p. 19.
   8. *E.W.*, II, vi.

causes.[9] But to understand more exactly what he means by this identification of philosophy with reasoning, we must consider three contrasts that run through all his writing: the contrast between philosophy and theology (reason and faith), between philosophy and "science" (reason and empiricism), and between philosophy and experience (reason and sense).

Reasoning is concerned solely with causes and effects. It follows, therefore, that its activity must lie within a world composed of things that are causes or the effects of causes. If there is another way of conceiving this world, it is not within the power of reasoning to follow it; if there are things by definition causeless or ingenerable, they belong to a world other than that of philosophy. This at once, for Hobbes, excludes from philosophy the consideration of the universe as a whole, things infinite, things eternal, final causes and things known only by divine grace or revelation: it excludes what Hobbes comprehensively calls theology and faith. He denies, not the existence of these things, but their rationality.[10] This method of circumscribing the concerns of philosophy is not, of course, original in Hobbes. It has roots that go back to Augustine, if not further, and it was inherited by the seventeenth century (where one side of it was distinguished as the heresy of Fideism: both Montaigne and Pascal were Fideists) directly from its formulation in the Averroism of Scotus and Occam. Indeed, this doctrine is one of the seeds in scholasticism from which modern philosophy sprang. Philosophical explanation, then, is concerned with things caused. A world of such things is, necessarily, a world from which teleology is excluded; its internal movement comprises the impact of its parts upon one another, of attraction and repulsion, not of growth or development. It is a world conceived on the analogy of a machine, where to explain an effect we go to its immediate cause, and to seek the

9. *E.W.*, I, 65–66, 387.
10. *L.*, p. 80; *E.W.*, I, 10, 410.

result of a cause we go only to its immediate effect.[11] In other words, the mechanistic element in Hobbes's philosophy is derived from his rationalism; its source and authority lie, not in observation, but in reasoning. He does not say that the natural world is a machine; he says only that the rational world is analogous to a machine. He is a scholastic, not a "scientific" mechanist. This does not mean that the mechanistic element is unimportant in Hobbes; it means only that it is derivative. It is, indeed, of the greatest importance, for Hobbes's philosophy is, in all its parts, preeminently a philosophy of *power* precisely because philosophy is reasoning, reasoning the elucidation of mechanism, and mechanism essentially the combination, transfer, and resolution of forces. The end of philosophy itself is power—*scientia propter potentiam*.[12] Man is a complex of powers; desire is the desire for power, pride is illusion about power, honour opinion about power, life the unremitting exercise of power, and death the absolute loss of power. And the civil order is conceived as a coherence of powers, not because politics is vulgarly observed to be a competition of powers, or because civil philosophy must take its conceptions from natural philosophy, but because to subject the civil order to rational enquiry unavoidably turns it into a mechanism.

In the writings of Hobbes, philosophy and science are not contrasted *eo nomine*. Such a contrast would have been impossible in the seventeenth century, with its absence of differentiation between the sciences and its still unshaken hold on the conception of the unity of human knowledge. Indeed, Hobbes normally uses the word science as a synonym for philosophy; rational knowledge is scientific knowledge. Nevertheless, Hobbes is near the beginning of a new view of the structure and parts of knowledge, a change of view which became clearer in the gener-

11. *E.W.*, II, xiv.
12. *E.W.*, I, xiv; *O.L.*, I, 6.

ation of Locke and was completed by Kant. Like Bacon and others before him, Hobbes has his own classification of the *genres* of knowledge,[13] and that it is a classification which involves a distinction between philosophy and what we have come to call "science" is suggested by his ambiguous attitude to the work of contemporary scientists. He wrote with an unusually generous enthusiasm of the great advances made by Kepler, Galileo, and Harvey; "the beginning of astronomy," he says, "is not to be derived from farther time than from Copernicus";[14] but he had neither sympathy nor even patience for the "new or experimental philosophy," and he did not conceal his contempt for the work of the Royal Society, founded in his lifetime. But this ambiguity ceases to be paradoxical when we see what Hobbes was about, when we understand that one of the few internal tensions of his thought arose from an attempted but imperfectly achieved distinction between science and philosophy. The distinction, well known to us now, is that between knowledge of things as they appear and enquiry into the fact of their appearing, between a knowledge (with all the necessary assumptions) of the phenomenal world and a theory of knowledge itself. Hobbes appreciated this distinction, and his appreciation of it allies him with Locke and with Kant and separates him from Bacon and even Descartes. He perceived that his concern as a philosopher was with the second and not the first of these enquiries; yet the distinction remained imperfectly defined in his mind. But that philosophy meant for Hobbes something different from the enquiries of natural science is at once apparent when we consider the starting-place of his thought and the character of the questions he thinks it necessary to ask. He begins with sensation; and he begins there, not because there is no deceit or crookedness in the utterances of the senses, but because the fact of our having sensations seems to him the only thing of which we can be indu-

13. *L.,* p. 64.
14. *E.W.,* I, viii.

bitably certain.[15] And the question he asks himself is, what *must* the world be like for us to have the sensations we undoubtedly experience? His enquiry is into the cause of sensation, an enquiry to be conducted, not by means of observation, but by means of reasoning. And if the answer he proposes owes something to the inspiration of the scientists, that does nothing to modify the distinction between science and philosophy inherent in the question itself. For the scientist of his day the world of nature was almost a machine, Kepler had proposed the substitution of the word *vis* for the word *anima* in physics; and Hobbes, whose concern was with the rational world (by definition also conceived as the analogy of a machine), discovered that some of the general ideas of the scientists could be turned to his own purposes. But these pardonable appropriations do nothing to approximate his enquiry to that of Galileo or Newton. Philosophy is reasoning, this time contrasted, not with theology, but with what we have come to know as natural science. And the question, What, in an age of science, is the task of philosophy? which was to concern the nineteenth century so deeply, was already familiar to Hobbes. And it is a false reading of his intention and his achievement which finds in his civil philosophy the beginning of sociology or a science of politics, the beginning of that movement of thought that came to regard "the methods of physical science as the proper models for political."[16]

But the contrast that finally distinguishes philosophy and reveals its full character is that between philosophy and what Hobbes calls experience. For in elucidating this distinction Hobbes shows us philosophy coming into being, shows it as a thing generated and relates it to its cause, thereby establishing it as itself a proper subject of rational consideration. The mental history of a man begins with sensation, "for there is no concep-

15. It will be remembered that the brilliant and informal genius of Montaigne had perceived that our most certain knowledge is what we know about ourselves, and had made of this a philosophy of introspection.

16. J. S. Mill, *Autobiography*, p. 165.

tion in a man's mind, which hath not at first, totally, or by parts, been begotten upon the organs of sense."[17] Some sensations, perhaps, occupying but an instant, involve no reference to others and no sense of time. But commonly, sensations, requiring a minimum time of more than a single instant, and reaching a mind already stored with the relics of previous sensations, are impossible without that which gives a sense of time—memory.[18] Sensation involves recollection, and a man's experience is nothing but the recollected after-images of sensations. But from his power to remember man derives another power, imagination, which is the ability to recall and turn over in the mind the decayed relics of past sensation, the ability to experience even when the senses themselves have ceased to speak. Moreover imagination, though it depends on past sensations, is not an entirely servile faculty; it is capable of compounding together relics of sensations felt at different times. Indeed, in imagination we may have in our minds images not only of what we have never actually seen (as when we imagine a golden mountain though we have seen only gold and a mountain), but even of what we could never see, such as a chimera. But imagination remains servile in that "we have no transition from one imagination to another whereof we never had the like before in our senses."[19] Two things more belong to experience; the fruits of experience. The first is History, which is the ordered register of past experiences. The second is prudence, which is the power to anticipate experience by means of the recollection of what has gone before. "Of our conceptions of the past, we make a future."[20] A full, well-recollected experience gives the "foresight" and "wisdom" that belong to the prudent man, a wisdom that springs from the appreciation of those causes and effects that time and not reason teaches us. This is the end and crown of experience. In the mind

17. *L.,* p. 11.
18. *E.W.,* I, 393.
19. *L.,* p. 18.
20. *E.W.,* IV, 16.

of the prudent or sagacious man, experience appears as a kind of knowledge. Governed by sense, it is necessarily individual, a particular knowledge of particulars. But, within its limits, it is "absolute knowledge";[21] there is no ground upon which it can be doubted, and the categories of truth and falsehood do not apply to it. It is mere, uncritical "knowledge of fact": "experience concludeth nothing universal."[22] And in all its characteristics it is distinguished from philosophical knowledge, which (because it is reasoned) is general and not particular, a knowledge of consequences and not of facts, and conditional and not absolute.

Our task now is to follow Hobbes in his account of the generation of rational knowledge from experience. In principle, experience (except perhaps when it issues in history) is something man shares with animals and has only in a greater degree: memory and imagination are the unsought mechanical products of sensation, like the movements that continue on the surface of water after what disturbed it has sunk to rest. In order to surmount the limits of this sense-experience and achieve reasoned knowledge of our sensations, we require not only to have sensations, but to be conscious of having them; we require the power of introspection. But the cause of this power must lie in sense itself, if the power is to avoid the imputation of being an easy *deus ex machina*. Language satisfies both these conditions: it makes introspection possible, and springs from a power we share with animals, the physical power of making sounds. For, though language "when disposed of in speech and pronounced to others"[23] is the means whereby men declare their thoughts to one another, it is primarily the only means by which a man may communicate his own thoughts to himself, may become conscious of the contents of his mind. The beginning of language is giving names to after-images of sensations and thereby becoming conscious of them; the act of naming the image is the act of becoming conscious of

21. *L.*, p. 64.
22. *E.W.*, IV, 18.
23. *E.W.*, I, 16.

it. For, "a name is a word taken at pleasure to serve as a mark that may raise in our minds a thought like some thought we had before."[24]

Language, the giving of names to images, is not itself reasonable, it is the arbitrary precondition of all reasoning:[25] the generation of rational knowledge is by words out of experience. The achievement of language is to "register our thoughts," to fix what is essentially fleeting. And from this achievement follows the possibility of definition, the conjunction of general names, proposition, and rational argument, all of which consist in the "proper use of names in language." But, though reasoning brings with it knowledge of the general and the possibility of truth and its opposite, absurdity,[26] it can never pass beyond the world of names. Reasoning is nothing else but the addition and subtraction of names, and "gives us conclusions, not about the nature of things, but about the names of things. That is to say, by means of reason we discover only whether the connections we have established between names are in accordance with the arbitrary convention we have established concerning their meanings."[27] This is at once a nominalist and a profoundly sceptical doctrine. Truth is of universals, but they are names, the names of images left over from sensations; and a true proposition is not an assertion about the real world. We can, then, surmount the limits of sense-experience and achieve rational knowledge; and it is this knowledge, with its own severe limitations, that is the concern of philosophy.

But philosophy is not only knowledge of the universal, it is a knowledge of causes. Informally, Hobbes describes it as "the natural reason of man flying up and down among the creatures, and

---

24. *E.W.*, I, 16.

25. This is why introspection that falls short of reasoning is possible. *E.W.*, I, 73.

26. Since truth is of propositions, its opposite is a statement that is absurd or nonsensical. Error belongs to the world of experience and is a failure in foresight. *L.*, p. 34.

27. *O.L.*, V, 257.

bringing back a true report of their order, causes and effects."[28] We have seen already how, by limiting philosophy to a knowledge of things caused (because reasoning itself must observe this limit) he separates it from theology. We have now to consider why he believed that the essential work of reasoning (and therefore of philosophy) was the demonstration of the cause of things caused. Cause for Hobbes is the means by which anything comes into being. Unlike any of the Aristotelian causes, it is essentially that which, previous in time, brings about the effect. A knowledge of cause is, then, a knowledge of how a thing is generated.[29] But why must philosophy be a knowledge of this sort? Hobbes's answer would appear to be, first, that this sort of knowledge can spring from reasoning while it is impossible to mere experience, and, secondly, that since, *ex hypothesi*, the data of philosophy are effects, the only possible enlargement of our knowledge of them must consist in a knowledge of their causes. If we add to the experience of an effect a knowledge of its generation, a knowledge of its "constitutive cause,"[30] we know everything that may be known. In short, a knowledge of causes is the pursuit in philosophy because philosophy is reasoning.[31]

The third characteristic of philosophical knowledge, as distinguished from experience, is that it is conditional, not absolute. Hobbes's doctrine is that when, in reasoning, we conclude that the cause of something is such and such, we can mean no more than that such and such is a possible efficient cause, and not that it is the actual cause. There are three criteria by which a suggested cause may be judged, and proof that the cause actually operated is not among them. For reasoning, a cause must be "imaginable," the necessity of the effect must be shown to follow from the cause, and it must be shown that nothing false (that is,

28. *E.W.*, I, xiii.
29. *E.W.*, VII, 78.
30. *E.W.*, II, xiv.
31. Hobbes gives the additional reason that a knowledge of causes is useful to mankind. *E.W.*, I, 7–10.

not present in the effect) can be derived.[32] And what satisfies
these conditions may be described as an hypothetical efficient
cause. That philosophy is limited to the demonstration of such
causes is stated by Hobbes on many occasions; it applies not only
to the detail of his philosophy, but also to the most general of all
causes, to body and motion. For example, when he says that the
cause or generation of a circle is "the circumduction of a body
whereof one end remains unmoved," he adds that this gives
"some generation [of the figure], though perhaps not that by
which it was made, yet that by which it might have been made."[33]
And when he considers the general problem of the cause of sensations, he concludes, not with the categorical statement that
body and motion are the only causal existents, but that body (that
is, that which is independent of thought and which fills a portion
of space) and motion are the hypothetical efficient causes of our
having sensations. If there were no body there could be no motion, and if there were no motion of bodies there could be no
sensation; *sentire semper idem et non sentire ad idem recidunt.*[34]
From beginning to end there is no suggestion in Hobbes that
philosophy is anything other than conditional knowledge, knowledge of hypothetical generations and conclusions about the
names of things, not about the nature of things.[35] With these
philosophy must be satisfied, though they are but fictions. Indeed, philosophy may be defined as the establishment by reasoning of true fictions. And the ground of this limitation is, that
the world being what it is, reasoning can go no further. "There
is no effect which the power of God cannot produce in many
several ways,"[36] verification *ad oculos* is impossible because

32. *Elements of Law*, Appendix II, § 1, 168.
33. *E.W.*, I, 6, 386–87.
34. *O.L.*, I, 321.
35. *L.*, pp. 49–50.
36. *E.W.*, VII, 3. It may be observed that what is recognized here is the normally
unstated presupposition of all seventeenth-century science: the Scotist belief that
the natural world is the creation *ex nihilo* of an omnipotent God, and that therefore
categorical knowledge of its detail is not deducible but (if it exists) must be the prod-

these causes are rational not perceptible, and consequently the farthest reach of reason is the demonstration of causes which satisfy the three rational criteria.

My contention is, then, that the system of Hobbes's philosophy lies in his conception of the nature of philosophical knowledge, and not in any doctrine about the world. And the inspiration of his philosophy is the intention to be guided by reason and to reject all other guides: this is the thread, the hidden thought, that gives it coherence, distinguishing it from Faith, "Science," and Experience. It remains to guard against a possible error. The lineage of Hobbes's rationalism lies, not (like that of Spinoza or even Descartes) in the great Platonic-Christian tradition, but in the sceptical, late scholastic tradition. He does not normally speak of Reason, the divine illumination of the mind that unites man with God; he speaks of reasoning. And he is not less persuaded of its fallibility and limitations than Montaigne himself.[37] By means of reasoning we certainly pass beyond mere sense-experience, but when imagination and prudence have generated rational knowledge, they do not, like drones, perish; they continue to perform in human life functions that reasoning itself cannot discharge. Nor, indeed, is man, in Hobbes's view, primarily a reasoning creature. This capacity for general hypothetical reasoning distinguishes him from the animal, but he remains fundamentally a creature of passion, and it is by passion not less than by reasoning that he achieves his salvation.[38]

We have considered Hobbes's view of philosophy because civil philosophy, whatever else it is, is philosophy. Civil philosophy, the subject of *Leviathan,* is precisely the application of this conception of philosophy to civil association. It is not the last chapter in a philosophy of materialism, but the reflection of civil associa-

---

uct of observation. Characteristically adhering to the tradition, Hobbes says that the only thing we can know of God is his omnipotence.

37. *L.,* p. 34.
38. *L.,* p. 98.

tion in the mirror of a rationalistic philosophy. But if the *genus* of civil philosophy is its character as philosophy, its *differentia* is derived from the matter to be considered. Civil philosophy is settling the generation or constitutive cause of civil association. And the kind of hypothetical efficient cause that civil philosophy may be expected to demonstrate is determined by the fact that civil association is an artifact: it is artificial, not natural. Now, to assert that civil association is an artifact is already to have settled the question of its generation, and Hobbes himself does not begin with any such assertion. His method is to establish the artificial character of civil association by considering its generation. But in order to avoid false expectations it will be wise for us to anticipate the argument and consider what he means by this distinction between art and nature.

Hobbes has given us no collected account of his philosophy of artifice; it is to be gathered only from scattered observations. But when these are put together, they compose a coherent view. A work of art is the product or effect of mental activity. But this in itself does not distinguish it securely from nature, because the universe itself must be regarded as the product of God's mental activity, and what we call "nature" is to God an artifact;[39] and there are products of human mental activity which, having established themselves, become for the observer part of his natural world. More firmly defined, then, a work of art is the product of mental activity considered from the point of view of its cause. And, since what we have to consider are works of human art, our enquiry must be into the kind of natural human mental activity that may result in a work of art; for the cause of a work of art must lie in nature; that is, in experience. It would appear that the activities involved are willing and reasoning. But reasoning itself is artificial, not natural; it is an "acquired" not a "native" mental activity,[40] and therefore cannot be considered as part of

39. *L.*, p. 5.
40. *L.*, p. 29.

the generation of a work of art.[41] We are left, then, with willing, which, belonging to experience and not reasoning, is undoubtedly a natural mental activity. The cause (hypothetical and efficient, of course) of a human work of art is the will of a man. And willing is "the last desire in deliberating," deliberating being mental discourse in which the subject is desires and aversions.[42] It is a creative activity (not merely imitative), in the same way as imagination, working on sensations, creates a new world of hitherto separated parts. Both will and imagination are servile only in that their products must be like nature in respect of being mechanisms; that is, complexes of cause and effect.[43] Moreover, will creates not only when it is single and alone, but also in concert with other wills. The product of an agreement between wills is no less a work of art than the product of one will. And the peculiarity of civil association, as a work of art, is its generation from a number of wills. The word "civil," in Hobbes, means artifice springing from more than one will. Civil history (as distinguished from natural history) is the register of events that have sprung from the voluntary actions of man in commonwealths.[44] Civil authority is authority arising out of an agreement of wills, while natural authority (that of the father in the family) has no such generation and is consequently of a different character.[45] And civil association is itself contrasted on this account with the appearance of it in mere natural gregariousness.[46]

Now, with this understanding of the meaning of both "civil" and "philosophical," we may determine what is to be expected for a civil philosophy. Two things may be expected from it. First, it will exhibit the internal mechanism of civil association as a sys-

41. The expression "natural reason" is not absent from Hobbes's writings, but it means the reasoning of individual men contrasted with the doubly artificial reasoning of the artificial man, the Leviathan, e.g. *L.*, pp. 5, 42, 233, 242; *E.W.*, I, xiii.

42. *L.*, p. 38.
43. *L.*, p. 8.
44. *L.*, p. 64.
45. *L.*, p. 153.
46. *L.*, p. 130.

tem of cause and effect and settle the generation of the parts of
civil association. And secondly, we may expect it to settle the
generation, in terms of an hypothetical efficient cause, of the
artifact as a whole; that is, to show this work of art springing
from the specific nature of man. But it may be observed that two
courses lie open to anyone, holding the views of Hobbes, who
undertakes this project. Philosophy, we have seen, may argue
from a given effect to its hypothetical efficient cause, or from a
given cause to its possible effect. Often the second form of argument is excluded; this is so with sensations, when the given is an
effect and the cause is to seek. But in civil philosophy, and in all
reasoning concerned with artifacts, both courses are open; for
the cause and the effect (human nature and civil association) are
both given, and the task of philosophy is to unite the details of
each to each in terms of cause and effect. Hobbes tells us[47] that
his early thinking on the subject took the form of an argument
from effect (civil association) to cause (human nature), from art
to nature; but it is to be remarked that, not only in *Leviathan*,
but also in all other accounts he gives of his civil philosophy, the
form of the argument is from cause to effect, from nature to art.
But, since the generation is rational and not physical, the direction from which it is considered is clearly a matter of indif-
ference.

V. The Argument of *Leviathan*

Any account worth giving of the argument of *Leviathan* must be
an interpretation; and this account, because it is an interpretation, is not a substitute for the text. Specific comment is avoided;
but the implicit comment involved in selection, emphasis, the
alteration of the language, and the departure from the order of
ideas in the text cannot be avoided.

47. *E.W.*, II, vi, xiv.

The nature of man is the predicament of mankind. A knowledge of this nature is to be had from introspection, each man reading himself in order to discern in himself, mankind. Civil philosophy begins with this sort of knowledge of the nature of man.[48]

Man is a creature of sense. He can have nothing in his mind that was not once a sensation. Sensations are movements in the organs of sense which set up consequent movements in the brain; after the stimulus of sense has spent itself, there remain in the mind slowly fading relics of sensations, called images or ideas. Imagination is the consciousness of these images; we imagine what was once in the senses but is there no longer. Memory is the recollection of these images. A man's experience is the whole contents of his memory, the relics of sensations available to him in recollection. And Mental Discourse is images succeeding one another in the mind. This succession may be haphazard or it may be regulated, but it always follows some previous succession of sensations. A typical regulated succession of images is where the image of an effect calls up from memory the image of its cause. Mental discourse becomes Prudence or foresight when, by combining the recollection of the images of associated sensations in the past with the present experience of one of the sensations, we anticipate the appearance of the others. Prudence is natural wisdom. All these together may be called the *receptive* powers of a man. Their cause is sensation (into the cause of which we need not enquire here), and they are nothing other than movements in the brain.[49]

But, springing from these there is another set of movements in the brain, which may be called comprehensively the *active*

48. Man is a mechanism; but a mechanism may be considered at different levels of abstraction. For example, the working of a watch may be described mathematically in terms of quantities, or in the mechanical terms of force and inertia, or in terms of its visible parts, springs, and cogs. And to choose one level does not deny the possibility of the others. In selecting introspection as the sort of knowledge of man required in civil philosophy, Hobbes is doing no more than to choose what he considers to be the relevant level of abstraction.

49. *L.*, chs. i–iii.

powers of a man; his emotions or passions. These movements
are called voluntary to distinguish them from involuntary movements such as the circulation of the blood. Voluntary activity is
activity in response to an idea, and therefore it has its beginning
in imagination. Its undifferentiated form is called Endeavour,
which, when it is towards the image from which it sprang is
called Desire or Appetite, and when it is away from its originat-
ing image is called Aversion. Love corresponds to Desire; Hate
to Aversion. And whatever is the object of a man's desire he calls
Good, and whatever he hates he calls Evil. There is, therefore,
nothing good or evil as such; for different men desire different
things, each calling the object of his desire good, and the same
man will, at different times, love and hate the same thing. Pleasure is a movement in the mind that accompanies the image of
what is held to be good, pain one that accompanies an image
held to be evil. Now, just as the succession of images in the mind
is called Mental Discourse (the end of which is Prudence), so
the succession of emotions in the mind is called Deliberation,
the end of which is Will. While desire and aversion succeed one
another without any decision being reached, we are said to be
deliberating; when a decision is reached, and desire is concen-
trated upon some object, we are said to will it. Will is the last
desire in deliberating. There can, then, be no final end, no *summum bonum*,[50] for a man's active powers; human conduct is not
teleological, it is concerned with continual success in obtaining
those things which a man from time to time desires, and success
lies not only in procuring what is desired, but also in the assurance that what will in the future be desired will also be procured.
This success is called Felicity, which is a condition of movement,
not of rest or tranquillity. The means by which a man may obtain
this success are called, comprehensively, his Power; and there-

---

50. There is, however, a *summum malum,* and it is death; its opposite, being alive,
is only a "primary good." *L.,* p. 75; *O.L.,* II, 98.

fore there is in man a perpetual and restless desire for power, because power is the *conditio sine qua non* of Felicity.[51]

The receptive and the active powers of man derive directly from the possession of the five senses; the senses are their efficient cause. And since we share our senses with the animals, we share also these powers. Men and beasts do not have the same images and desires; but both alike have imagination and desire. What then, since this does not, differentiates man from beast? Two things: religion and the power of reasoning. Both these are at once natural and artificial: they belong to the nature of man because their generation is in sense and emotion, but they are artificial because they are the products of human mental activity. Religion and reasoning are mankind's natural inheritance of artifice.

The character of reasoning and its generation from the invention of speech has already been described. Here it need only be added that, just as Prudence is the end-product of imagination and Felicity of emotion, so Sapience is the end-product of reasoning; and Sapience is a wealth of general hypothetical conclusions or theorems, found out by reasoning, about the causes and consequences of the names of sensations.[52]

The seed of religion, like that of reasoning, is in the nature of man, though what springs from that seed, a specific set of religious beliefs and practices, is an artifact. The generation of religion is the necessary defect of Prudence, the inexperience of man. Prudence is foresight of a probable future based upon recollection, and insight into a probable cause also based upon recollection. Its immediate emotional effect is to allay anxiety and fear, fear of an unknown cause or consequence.[53] But since its range is necessarily limited, it has the additional effect of increasing man's fear of what lies beyond that limit. Prudence, in

51. *L.*, chs. vi, xi.
52. *L.*, chs. iv, v.
53. For Hobbes, fear is aversion from something believed to be hurtful. *L.*, p. 43.

restricting the area in the control of fear, increases the fear of what is still to be feared; having some foresight, men are all the more anxious because that foresight is not complete. (Animals, having little or no foresight, suffer only the lesser evil of its absence, not the greater of its limitation.) Religion is the product of mental activity to meet this situation. It springs from prudent fear of what is beyond the power of prudence to find out,[54] and is the worship of what is feared because it is not understood. Its contradictory is Knowledge; its contrary is Superstition, worship springing from fear of what is properly an object of knowledge. The perpetual fear that is the spring of religion seeks an object on which to concentrate itself, and calls that object God. It is true that perseverance in reasoning may reveal the necessity of a First Cause, but so little can be known about it that the attitude of human beings towards it must always be one of worship rather than knowledge. And each man, according to the restriction of his experience and the greatness of his fear, renders to God worship and honour.[55]

The human nature we are considering is the internal structure and powers of the individual man, a structure and powers which would be his even if he were the only example of his species: we are considering the character of the solitary. He lives in the world of his own sensations and imaginations, desires and aversions, prudence, reason, and religion. For his thoughts and actions he is answerable to none but himself. He is conscious of possessing certain powers, and the authority for their exercise lies in nothing but their existence, and that authority is absolute. Consequently, an observer from another world, considering the character of our solitary, would not improperly attribute to him a natural freedom or right of judgement in the exercise of his powers of mind and body for the achievement of the ends given

54. *L.*, p. 82. The limitations of reasoning also produce fear, a rational fear of what is beyond the power of reason to discern.

55. *L.*, ch. xii.

in his nature.[56] In the pursuit of felicity he may make mistakes, in his mental discourse he may commit errors, in his reasoning he may be guilty of absurdity, but a denial of the propriety of the pursuit would be a meaningless denial of the propriety of his character and existence. Further, when our solitary applies his powers of reasoning to find out fit means to attain the ends dictated by his emotional nature, he may, if his reasoning is steady, light upon some general truths or theorems with regard to the probable consequences of his actions. It appears, then, that morally unfettered action (which may be called a man's natural right to exercise his natural powers), and the possibility of formulating general truths about the pursuit of felicity, are corollaries of human nature.

Two further observations may be made. First, in the pursuit of felicity certain habits of mind and action will be found to be specially serviceable, and these are called Virtues. Other habits will hinder the pursuit, and these are called Defects. Defects are misdirected virtues. For example, prudence in general is a virtue, but to be overprudent, to look too far ahead and allow too much care for the future, reduces a man to the condition of Prometheus on the rock (whose achievements by night were devoured by the anxieties of the day), and inhibits the pursuit.[57] And the preeminently inhibiting defect from which human beings may be observed to suffer is Pride. This is the defect of Glory, and its other names are Vanity and Vainglory. Glory, which is exultation in the mind based upon a true estimate of a man's powers to procure felicity, is a useful emotion; it is both the cause and effect of well-grounded confidence. But pride is a man's false estimate of his own powers, and is the forerunner of certain failure. Indeed, so fundamental a defect is pride, that it may be

56. Freedom, for Hobbes, can be properly attributed only to a body whose motion is not hindered. *L.*, p. 161. And the "right" derives, of course, not from the authority of a natural law, but from the character of the individual as an *ens completum*.

57. *L.*, p. 82.

taken as the type of all hindrances to the achievement of felicity.[58] Secondly, it may be observed that death, the involuntary cessation of desire and the pursuit which is the end of desire, is the thing of all others the most hateful; it is the *summum malum*. And that which men hate they also fear if it is beyond their control. Prudence tells a man that he will die, and by taking thought the prudent man can sometimes avoid death by avoiding its probable occasions, and, so far, the fear of it will be diminished. But death will outdistance the fastest runner; in all its forms it is something to be feared as well as hated. Yet it is to be feared most when it is most beyond the control of prudence: the death to be most greatly feared is that which no foresight can guard against—sudden death.[59] It would appear, then, that Pride is the type of all hindrances to the achievement of felicity, and death the type of all Aversion.

Now, the element of unreality in the argument so far is not that the solitary, whose character we have been considering, is an abstraction and does not exist (he does exist and he is the real individual man), but that he does not exist alone. This fact, that there is more than one of his kind, must now be recognized; we must turn from the nature of man to consider the natural condition of man. And it is at this point that the predicament of mankind becomes apparent; for, apart from mortality, the character of the solitary man presents nothing that could properly be called a predicament.

The existence of others of his kind, and the impossibility of escaping their company, is the first real impediment in the pursuit of felicity; for another man is necessarily a competitor. This

---

58. *L.*, pp. 44, 88.

59. In *Leviathan* death itself is taken to be the greatest evil; the refinement about sudden death is an interpretation of the view that appears in the *De Cive* and elsewhere that the greatest evil is *violent* death at the hands of another. This not only terminates the pursuit of felicity, but does so in a manner shameful to the victim; it convicts him of inferiority.

is no mere observation, though its effects may be seen by any candid observer; it is a deduction from the nature of felicity. For, whatever appears to a man to belong to his felicity he must strive for with all his powers, and men who strive for the possession of the same object are enemies of one another. Moreover, he who is most successful will have the most enemies and be in the greatest danger. To have built a house and cultivated a garden is to have issued an invitation to all others to take it by force, for it is against the common view of felicity to weary oneself with making what can be acquired by less arduous means. And further, competition does not arise merely when two or more happen to want the same thing, for when a man is among others of his kind his felicity is not absolute but comparative; and since a large part of it comes from a feeling of superiority, of having more than his fellow, the competition is essential, not accidental. There is, at best, a permanent potential enmity between men, "a perpetual contention for Honour, Riches, and Authority."[60] And to make matters worse, each man is so nearly the equal of each other man in power, that superiority of strength (which might set some men above the disadvantage of competition: the possibility of losing) is nothing better than an illusion. The natural condition of man is one of the competition of equals for the things (necessarily scarce because of the desire for *superiority*)[61] that belong to felicity. But equality of power, bringing with it, not only equality of fear, but also equality of hope, will urge every man to try to outwit his neighbour. And the end is open conflict, a war of all against all, in which the defects of man's character and circumstances make him additionally vulnerable. For, if pride, the excessive estimate of his own powers, hinders a man in choosing the best course when he is alone, it will be the most crippling of all handicaps when played upon by a competitor in the race. And in a company of enemies, death, the *summum malum*, will be

60. *L.*, p. 547.
61. *L.*, p. 130.

closer than felicity. When a man is among men, pride is more dangerous and death more likely.[62]

But further, the relationship between these self-moved seekers after felicity is complicated by an ambiguity. They are enemies but they also need one another. And this for two reasons: without others there is no recognition of superiority and therefore no notable felicity; and many, perhaps most of the satisfactions which constitute a man's felicity are in the responses he may wring from others. The pursuit of felicity, in respect of a large part of it, is a procedure of bargaining with others in which one seeks what another has got and for which he must offer a satisfaction in return.

The predicament may now be stated precisely. There is a radical conflict between the nature of man and the natural condition of mankind: what the one urges with hope of achievement, the other makes impossible. Man is solitary; would that he were alone. For the sweetness of all he may come by through the efforts of others is made bitter by the price he must pay for it, and it is neither sin nor depravity that creates the predicament; nature itself is the author of his ruin.

But, like the seeds of fire (which were not themselves warm) that Prometheus brought mankind, like the first incipient movements (hardly to be called such) that Lucretius, and after him Hobbes, supposes to precede visible movement, the deliverance lies in the womb of nature. The saviour is not a visitor from another world, nor is it some godlike power of Reason come to create order out of chaos; there is no break either in the situation or in the argument. The remedy of the disease is homeopathic.[63]

The precondition of the deliverance is the recognition of the predicament. Just as, in Christian theory, the repentance of the sinner is the first indispensable step towards forgiveness and salvation, so here, mankind must first purge itself of the illusion

62. *L.*, ch. xiii.
63. *L.*, p. 98.

called pride. So long as a man is in the grip of this illusion he will hope to succeed tomorrow where he failed today; and the hope is vain. The purging emotion (for it is to emotion that we go to find the beginning of deliverance) is fear of death. This fear illuminates prudence; man is a creature civilized by fear of death. And what is begun in prudence is continued in reasoning; art supplements the gifts of nature.

For, as reasoning may find out truths for the guidance of a man in his pursuit of felicity when he is alone, so it is capable of uncovering similar truths in respect of his competitive endeavour to satisfy his wants. And since what threatens to defeat every attempt to procure felicity in these circumstances is the unconditionally competitive character of the pursuit (or, in a word, war), these truths found out by reason for avoiding this defeat of all by all may properly be called the articles of Peace. Such truths, indeed, have been uncovered, and they are all conditions qualifying the competitive pursuit of felicity which, if they are observed by all, will enhance the certainty, if not the magnitude of the satisfaction of each. They are sometimes called the "laws of nature," but this is a misnomer except in special circumstances (to be considered later) when they are recognized to be the commands of a God or of a civil sovereign. Properly speaking, they are only theorems, the product of reasoning about what conduces to the optimum satisfaction of human wants.[64] And they are fruitless until they are transformed from mere theorems into maxims of human conduct and from maxims into laws; that is, until they are recognized as valid rules of conduct of known jurisdiction, to be subscribed to by all who fall within that jurisdiction and to which penalties for nonsubscription have been annexed and power to enforce them provided. But this transformation also lies within the scope of human art. Such rules of conduct are neither more nor less than the product of an agreement to recognize them as rules, and human beings en-

64. *L.*, 122, 205.

dowed with the faculty of speech may not only communicate their thoughts to one another but also make agreements; indeed, their association is solely in terms of agreements. In short, moved by fear of ill-success in procuring the satisfaction of their wants, instructed by the conclusions of reasoning about how this ill-success may be mitigated, and endowed with the ability to set these conclusions to work, human beings enjoy the means of escaping from the predicament of mankind.

The substantial conclusions of human reasoning in this matter Hobbes sums up in a maxim: *do not that to another, which thou wouldest not have done to thyself.*[65] But, more important than this, is its formal message, namely, that where there is a multitude of men each engaged in unconditional competition with the others to procure the satisfaction of his own wants, and of roughly equal power to obtain each what he seeks, they may succeed in their respective endeavours only when its unconditionality is abated. The abrogation of the competition is, of course, impossible; there can be no common or communal felicity to which they might be persuaded to turn their attention. But this race, in which each seeks to come first and is also unavoidably and continuously fearful of not doing so, must have some rules imposed upon it if it is not to run everyone into the ground. And this can be done only in an agreement of those concerned.

Now, in the day-to-day transactions in which human beings seek the satisfaction of their wants this message of reason may often be listened to and acted upon. They make *ad hoc* agreements about procedures of bargaining, they enter into formal relationships, they even make and accept promises about future actions and often keep them. And although such arrangements cannot increase the magnitude of their felicity they may make its pursuit less chancy. But this abatement of uncertainty is at best marginal and at worst delusive. These *ad hoc* formal relationships of mutual agreement between assignable persons

65. *L.,* p. 121.

are evanescent; remotely they may reflect generally accepted theorems about rational conduct, but as rules they are the products of specific and temporary agreements between the persons concerned. And further, they are always liable to be undermined by the substantial relationship of competitive hostility. And even if such agreements contain penalty clauses for the nonobservance of the conditions they impose upon the conduct of a transaction, these (in the absence of an independent means of enforcing them) add nothing to the certainty of the sought-for outcome. And this is particularly the case where a promise to respond in the future is made by one who has already received a conditional benefit: the abatement of uncertainty it purports to offer depends upon the expectation of its being fulfilled, that is, upon whether or not it is in the interest of the respondent to keep his promise when the time comes to do so. And this, in Hobbes's view, must always be insufficiently certain for a reasonable man to bank upon it. In short, these *ad hoc* devices to increase the certainty of the satisfaction of wants, when taken alone, are themselves infected with uncertainty; where there is a present and substantial agreement about mutual interests they may be a convenience, where this is absent they provide merely an illusion of security.

What, then, is lacking here, and what is required for a "constant and lasting" release from the impediments which frustrate the common pursuit of individual felicity, is settled and known rules of conduct and a power sufficient to coerce those who fall within their jurisdiction to observe them. How may this condition of things be imagined to be "caused" or "generated"? First, it can be the effect only of an agreement among the human beings concerned. It is human beings associated in a particular manner, and all human association is by agreement. Secondly, it can be the effect of only a particular kind of agreement; namely, one in which a number of men, neither small nor unmanageably large, associate themselves in terms of a covenant to authorize an Actor to make standing rules to be subscribed to indifferently

in all their endeavours to satisfy their wants and to protect the
association from the hostile attentions of outsiders, and to endow
this Actor with power sufficient to enforce these conditions of
conduct and to provide this protection. Or, if this is not the only
imaginable cause of the desiderated condition of peace and security, then at least it is a possible cause.[66]

Such a covenant requires careful specification if it is to be
shown not itself to inhibit the pursuit of felicity and not to conflict with the alleged characters of those who enter into it. And
it is susceptible of various descriptions. It may, in general, be
recognized as an agreement of many to submit their wills every
one to the will of an Actor in respect of "all those things which
concern the common peace and safety."[67] More precisely it may
be identified as an agreement in which each participator surrenders his natural right to "govern himself" (or, "to be governed by
his own reason")[68] which derives from his natural right to the
unconditional pursuit of his own felicity. But if so, the character
of this surrender must be specified: it must be not a mere laying
down of this right, but a giving up of it to another. The right of
each to "govern himself" (that is, to determine the conditions
upon which he may pursue his felicity) is transferred to an Actor;
that is, to one authorized in the agreement to exercise it. But
who must this Actor be? Not a natural person, one among those
who covenant to surrender their right to govern themselves, for
that would be merely to place the government of their conduct
in the hands of one moved only by his appetite to satisfy his own
wants. The Actor is an artificial man who represents or "bears
the person" of each of those who, by agreeing among themselves
to do so, creates him and authorizes all his actions. What is created and authorized in this covenant is an Office which, although
it may be occupied by one or by more than one office-holder,
remains single and sovereign in all its official actions and utter-

66. *L.*, ch. xvii.
67. *L.*, p. 131.
68. *L.*, p. 99.

ances. Thus, the condition of peace and security is said to be the effect of "a covenant of every man with every man, in such manner, as if every man should say to every man, *I authorize and give up my right of governing myself, to this man, or to this assembly of men, on this condition, that thou give up thy right to him, and authorize all his actions in like manner.*"[69] Or again, it may be recognized as a covenant in which the covenanters agree among themselves "to confer all their strength and power upon one [artificial] man," thus providing the power to enforce recalcitrants to submit to the will and the judgement of an office-holder authorized to deliberate and to decide upon the conditions to be observed by all in their several adventures in pursuit of felicity. And here it is a covenant not merely to transfer a right (which could notionally be effected in a single once-for-all pronouncement), but to be continuously active in supplying the power required to exercise it—for the Office can have no such resources of its own.

This covenant, then, purports to create an artifact composed of a sovereign Ruler authorized and empowered by covenanters who thereby become "united in one person," transform themselves into Subjects and thus release themselves from the condition of war of all against all. This artifact is called a Commonwealth or *civitas.*

This is Hobbes's account of the hypothetical efficient cause of civil association. There are refinements I have not mentioned and, no doubt, also, difficulties; but the rest of the civil philosophy consists of an exhibition of this artifact as a system of internal causes and effects, joining where necessary parts of its structure to particular features of the predicament from which it is designed to rescue mankind. This may be conveniently considered under four heads: (1) the constitution of the sovereign authority, (2) the rights and "faculties" of the sovereign authority, (3) the obligations and liberties of subjects, (4) the civil condition.

69. *L.,* p. 131.

(1) The recipient of the transferred rights, whatever its constitution, is a single and sovereign authority. But this Office may be occupied by one or by many, and if by more than one either by some or by all. Thus a civil authority may have a monarchical, an aristocratic (or oligarchical), or a democratic constitution. Which it is to be is solely a matter of which is most likely to generate the peace for which civil association is instituted. The advantages of monarchy are obvious. But if the Office is occupied by an assembly of men, this cannot be because such an assembly is more likely to "represent" the variety of opinion among subjects, for a ruler is not the interpreter of the various wants of his subjects but the custodian of their will for peace. However, no kind of constitution is without its defects. Reason gives no conclusive answer, but tells us only that the main consideration is not wise but authoritative rule.[70]

(2) The rights of the occupant of the sovereign office are those which the covenanters confer upon him.[71] They are the right to rule and the right to enjoy the support of those who, in the agreement, have created themselves Subjects. These rights are both limited and unconditional. The covenanters have not surrendered their right to pursue felicity; they have surrendered only their right each to do this unconditionally, or (which is the same thing) on conditions which each decides for himself. But the rights with which they have endowed the sovereign are not retractable, and since he is not himself a party to any agreement he does not "bear their persons" on condition that he observes the terms of an agreement. Nor may any man exclude himself from the condition of Subject, on the grounds that he did not himself assent to the covenant, without declaring himself an "outlaw" and forfeiting the protection of the sovereign. The right to rule is the right to be the sole judge of what is necessary for the peace and security of subjects.

70. *L.*, ch. xix.
71. *L.*, ch. xviii.

The business of ruling is the exercise of this right. And the most important part of it is to make rules for the conduct of Subjects.[72] In a *civitas* the sovereign is the sole legislative authority; nothing is law save what he declares to be law, and it is law solely in virtue of that declaration. A law, in Hobbes's understanding of it, is a command, the expression of the Will of the Sovereign. Not every command of the sovereign is law, but only those commands which prescribe a rule of conduct to be subscribed to indifferently by all Subjects.

In general, the contents of civil law corresponds to the theorems which natural reason has uncovered about what conduces to peaceful relationships between human beings. In certain circumstances (with which we are not now concerned) these theorems may properly be called "natural laws" and the legal virtue or validity of the declarations of a civil sovereign may be thought to derive, at least in part, from their correspondence with these "natural laws"; but here the civil sovereign has nothing but theorems of natural reason to guide him and the legal validity of the rules he makes lies solely in their being his commands. In short, in civil association the validity of a law lies neither in the wisdom of the conditions it imposes upon conduct, nor even in its propensity to promote peace, but in its being the command of the sovereign and (although this is obscure) in its being effectively enforced. There may be unnecessary laws and even laws which increase rather than diminish contention, and these are to be deplored, but no valid law can, strictly speaking, be "unjust." "Just" conduct is identifiable only in terms of law and in civil association there is none but civil law. And if, as Hobbes suggests, the law which identifies the conditions upon which a man may rightfully call anything his own and upon which he may recognize the rights of others in this respect is the most important branch of civil law, this is because in each man coming to know what he may call his own and in being protected in his enjoy-

72. *L.*, p. 137, ch. xxvi.

ment of it the most fruitful cause of human contention is abated.[73]

Together with the right to make laws goes the right to interpret them, to administer them, and to punish those who do not observe them. All law requires interpretation; that is, decision about what it means in contingent circumstances. This decision must be authoritative. And, in Hobbes's view, laws lose all their virtue if their observance is not enforced by inescapable penalties. This "faculty" of the civil sovereign is exercised in courts of law presided over by himself or his agents. The sovereign's relationship to civil law is that as its maker he is *legibus solutus* (having unconditional authority to make or to repeal), but in respect of his judicial office he is bound by the law as it is. He may pardon some offences.[74]

Besides the sole right to make, repeal, interpret, administer, and enforce rules, the sovereign is the judge of what is necessary for the peace and security of his subjects in respect of threats to the association coming from without: the right to negotiate, make war, conclude peace, levy taxes to defray the expenses of war, and raise an army of volunteers of such dimensions as he shall think fit. He has the right to choose his own counsellors and agents, and he is himself the commander-in-chief of such military force as the association disposes.[75]

Lastly, the civil sovereign, although he cannot dictate the beliefs of his subjects, has the right to inspect and to govern all expressions of opinion or doctrine among his subjects (especially those addressed to large audiences) in relation to their propensity to promote or to disrupt the peace of the association. This censorship is not directly concerned with the truth or falsity of the opinions uttered, but "a doctrine repugnant to peace, can no

73. *L.*, pp. 111, 137.
74. *L.*, p. 137.
75. *L.*, pp. 137–38.

more be true, than peace and concord can be against the law of nature."[76]

It should be noted that the office of Sovereign has no rights of "lordship"; its *dominium* is solely *regale*.

(3) Civil Subjects are persons who, in a mutual agreement, have transferred the right of each to govern himself to a sovereign Actor; they have covenanted with one another to authorize all his actions, each to avouch every such action as his own, to submit their judgements and wills to his judgement and will in all that concerns their peace and security, to obey his commands, and to pledge all their strength and power to support the exercise of his authority. Thus, in a mutual agreement, they have each and all undertaken an obligation. Each in agreement with all others has bound himself in advance to a specified course of conduct in relation to one another and in relation to a ruler and his acts of ruling. In what respect may a civil Subject be said to be free?[77]

Freedom means the absence of external impediment to movement; and a man, whose movement is the performance of actions he has willed to perform, is properly said to be free when "in those things, which by his strength and wit he is able to do, [he] is not hindered to do what he has willed to do."[78] Human freedom is a quality of conduct itself, not of will. To find no external stop in doing what he has a will to do is to be a free man.

Cives, however, are subject to artificial impediments which stand in the way of their doing what they wish to do; namely, civil laws and the penalties which attach to not observing them, even the penalty of death, which is a stop to all conduct. They are in a situation of being compelled to do what they may not wish to do. And in this respect their freedom is curtailed.

But, it may be observed, first, that this situation is one of their

76. *L.*, p. 136, ch. xlii.
77. *L.*, ch. xxi.
78. *L.*, p. 161.

own choosing; they may have chosen it out of fear of the alternative (the perpetual and unregulated obstruction of their actions
by others), but this does not make the covenant any the less a
free action. Whatever impediments they suffer on this account
have been authorized by themselves. And further, their covenant
was an act designed to emancipate them from certain external
impediments to the pursuit of felicity, and if it were to be consci-
entiously observed by all there would be a net gain of freedom;
fewer and less disastrous impediments to their willed actions.

More to the point, however, are the following considerations.
Civil authority, the regulation of human conduct by law, does not
and cannot prescribe the whole of any man's conduct. Apart
from the fact that rules can be observed only in choosing to perform actions which they do not themselves prescribe, there is
always an area of the conduct of civil Subjects which, on account
of the silence of the law, they are free to occupy on their own
terms; to do and to forebear each at his own discretion. And the
"greatest liberty" of civil subjects derives from the silences of the
law.[79] Furthermore, civil subjects enjoy a freedom which Hobbes
calls their "true freedom," which derives from the precise form
of the covenant; in specifying their obligations the covenant
specifies also a freedom. Each covenanter has surrendered his
right to govern himself and has undertaken to *authorize* the actions of the sovereign ruler as if they were his own. The terms of
the covenant exclude, and are designed to exclude, any undertaking to surrender rights which cannot be given up without a
man risking the loss of all that he designed to protect in making
the covenant; that is, his pursuit of felicity and even his life.[80]
Thus, the covenanter authorizes the sovereign to arraign him before a court for an alleged breach of the law, but he has no obligation to accuse himself without the assurance of pardon. And
although, if convicted, he authorizes the infliction upon himself

79. *L.*, pp. 162, 168.
80. *L.*, p. 167.

of the lawful penalty, even the penalty of death, he is not obliged to kill himself or any other man. And it is in the enjoyment of all those rights which he has not surrendered that the "true freedom" of the Subject lies. Finally, although he cannot himself retract the authorization he has given, he retains the right to protect himself and his interests by such strength as he may have if the authorized ruler is no longer able to protect him.[81]

(4) The civil condition is an artifact. And since it is human beings associated in terms of the authorization of the decisions and the actions of a single Sovereign, Hobbes calls it an Artificial Man. It is association articulated in terms of settled and known laws which define the conditions of a "just" relationship between its members. And since "justice," strictly speaking, is a function of having rules which cannot be breached with impunity, and since in default of a *civitas* there are no rules with penalties annexed to them but only unconditional competition for the satisfaction of wants together with some theorems about how this competition might become more fruitful from which nothing more than general maxims of prudent conduct may be rationally derived, "justice" and the civil condition may be said to be coeval.

But if human beings may find in civil association a condition of "peace" in which the frustrations and anxieties of an unconditional competition between men for the satisfaction of wants are relieved, these are not the only anxieties they suffer and this is not the only "peace" they seek. They are dimly aware of inhabiting a world in which nothing happens without a cause and they think and speak of this world, metaphorically, as the "natural kingdom of God," the first or master cause of all that happens being identified as the will of this God. But they are acutely aware of their ignorance of the efficient causes of occurrences and of their consequent inability to move about this world with confidence, assured of achieving the satisfaction of their wants.

81. *L.*, p. 170.

They are gnawed by an anxiety, distinguishable from that which
arises from their lack of power to compete unconditionally with
their fellows, and they seek relief not only in a *pax civilis* but in
a *pax dei*. They attribute to this God nothing but what is "war-
ranted by natural reason," they acknowledge his power (indeed
his omnipotence), they do not (or should not) dishonour him by
disputing about his attributes, and they address him in utterances of worship—and all this in a design to ingratiate themselves with what they cannot control and thus abate their anxieties. In the civil condition this worship may be in secret and thus
of no concern to the civil sovereign, or by private men in the
hearing of others and thus subject to the conditions of civility.
But since a civil association is a many joined in the will and authorized actions of a Sovereign authority, it must display this
unity in the worship of this God. He is to be recognized and
honoured in a public *cultus* and in utterances and gestures determined by the civil Sovereign. In a *civitas* the *pax dei* is an
integral part of the *pax civilis*.[82]

Now, even an attentive reader might be excused if he supposed
that the argument of *Leviathan* would end here. Whatever our
opinion of the cogency of the argument, it would appear that
what was projected as a civil philosophy had now been fulfilled.
But such is not the view of Hobbes. For him it remains to purge
the argument of an element of unreality which still disfigures it.
And it is not an element of unreality that appears merely at this
point; it carries us back to the beginning, to the predicament
itself, and to get rid of it requires a readjustment of the entire
argument. It will be remembered that one element of unreality
in the conception of the condition of nature (that is, in the cause
of civil association) was corrected as soon as it appeared; the natural man was recognized to be, though solitary, not alone. But
what has remained so far unacknowledged is that the natural

82. *L.*, ch. xxi.

man is, not only solitary and not alone, but is also the devotee of
a positive religion; the religion attributed to him was something
less than he believed. How fundamental an oversight this was
we shall see in a moment; but first we may consider the defect
in the argument from another standpoint. In the earlier statement, the predicament was fully exhibited in its universal character, but (as Hobbes sees it) the particular form in which it
appeared to his time, the peculiar folly of his age, somehow
escaped from that generality; and to go back over the argument
with this in the forefront of his mind seemed to him a duty that
the civil philosopher owed to his readers. The project, then, of
the second half of the argument of *Leviathan* is, by correcting an
error in principle, to show more clearly the local and transitory
mischief in which the universal predicament of mankind appeared in the seventeenth century. And both in the conception
and in the execution of this project, Hobbes reveals, not only his
sensitiveness to the exigencies of his time, but also the medieval
ancestry of his way of thinking.

The Europe of his day was aware of three positive religions:
Christianity, the Jewish religion, and the Moslem. These, in the
language of the Middle Ages, were *leges*,[83] because what distinguished them was the fact that the believer was subject to a *law*,
the law of Christ, of Moses, or of Mahomet. And no traditionalist
would quarrel with Hobbes's statement that "religion is not philosophy, but law."[84] The consequence in civil life of the existence
of these "laws" was that every believer was subject to two laws—
that of his *civitas* and that of his religion: his allegiance was divided. This is the problem that Hobbes now considers with his
accustomed vigour and insight. It was a problem common to all
positive religions, but not unnaturally Hobbes's attention is con-
centrated upon it in relation to Christianity.[85]

The man, then, whose predicament we have to consider is, in

83. Cf. the *De Legibus* of William of Auvergne, Bishop of Paris, d. 1249.
84. *E.W.*, VII, 5.
85. *L.*, ch. xxxii.

addition to everything else, a Christian. And to be a Christian means to acknowledge obligation under the *law* of God. This is a real obligation, and not merely the shadow of one, because it is a real law—a command expressing the will of God. This law is to be found in the Scriptures. There are men who speak of the results of human reasoning as Natural Laws, but if we are to accept this manner of speaking we must beware of falling into the error of supposing that they are laws because they are rational. The results of natural reasoning are no more than uncertain theorems,[86] general conditional conclusions, unless and until they are transformed into laws by being shown to be the will of some authority. If, in addition to being the deliverance of reasoning, they can be shown to be the will and command of God, then and then only can they properly be called laws, natural or divine; and then and then only can they be said to create obligation.[87] But, as a matter of fact, all the theorems of reasoning with regard to the conduct of men in pursuit of felicity are to be found in the scriptures, laid down as the commands of God. Now, the conclusion of this is, that no proper distinction can be maintained between a Natural or Rational and a Revealed law. All law is revealed in the sense that nothing is law until it is shown to be the command of God by being found in the scriptures. It is true that the scriptures may contain commands not to be discovered by human reasoning and these, in a special sense, may be called revealed; but the theorems of reasoning are laws solely on account of being the commands of God, and therefore their authority is no different from that of the commands not penetrable by the light of reasoning. There is, then, only one law, Natural and Divine; and it is revealed in scripture.

But Scripture is an artifact. It is, in the first place, an arbitrary selection of writings called canonical by the authority that recognized them. And secondly, it is nothing apart from interpreta-

86. *E.W.*, IV, 285.
87. *L.*, p. 122; *E.W.*, IV, 285.

tion. Not only does the history of Christianity show that interpretation is necessary and has been various, but any consideration of the nature of knowledge that is not entirely perfunctory must conclude that "no line is possible between what has come to men and their interpretation of what has come to them."[88] Nothing can be more certain than that, if the law of God is revealed in scripture, it is revealed only in an interpretation of scripture.[89] And interpretation is a matter of authority; for, whatever part reasoning may play in the process of interpretation, what determines everything is the decision, *whose* reasoning shall interpret? And the far-reaching consequences of this decision are at once clear when we consider the importance of the obligations imposed by this law. Whoever has the authority to determine this law has supreme power over the conduct of men, "for every man, if he be in his wits, will in all things yield to that man an absolute obedience, by virtue of whose sentence he believes himself to be either saved or damned."[90]

Now, in the condition of nature there are two possible claimants to this authority to settle and interpret scripture and thus determine the obligations of the Christian man. First, each individual man may claim to exercise this authority on his own behalf. And this claim must at once be admitted. For, if it belongs to a man's natural right to do whatever he deems necessary to procure felicity, it will belong no less to this right to decide what he shall believe to be his obligations under the law natural and divine. In nature every man is "governed by his own reason."[91] But the consequences of this will be only to make more desperate the contentiousness of the condition of nature. There will be as many "laws" called Christian as there are men who call themselves Christian; and what men did formerly by natural right, they will do now on a pretended obligation to God. A man's

88. Hort, *The Way, the Truth and the Life*, p. 175.
89. *L.*, ch. xxxiii.
90. *E.W.*, II, 283–97.
91. *L.*, p. 99.

actions may thus become conscientious, but conscience will be only his own good opinion of his actions.[92] And to the secular war of nature will be added the fierceness of religious dispute. But secondly, the claim to be the authority to settle and interpret the scriptures may be made on behalf of a special spiritual authority, calling itself, for the purpose, a church. And a claim of this sort may be made either by a so-called universal church (when the claim will be to have authority to give an interpretation to be accepted by all Christians everywhere), or by a church whose authority is limited to less than the whole number of Christians. But, whatever the form of the claim, what we have to enquire into is the generation of the authority. Whence could such an authority be derived? We may dispose at once of the suggestion that any spiritual authority holds a divine commission to exercise such a faculty. There is no foundation in history to support such a suggestion; and even if there were, it could not give the necessary ground for the authority. For, such an authority could only come about by a transfer of natural right as a consequence of a covenant; this is the only possible cause of any authority whatever to order men. But we have seen already that a transfer of rights as a consequence of a covenant does not, and could not, generate a special spiritual authority to interpret scripture; it generates infallibly a civil society. A special spiritual authority for settling the law of God and Nature, cannot, then, exist; and where it appears to exist, what really exists is only the natural authority of one man (the proper sphere of which is that man's own life) illegitimately extended to cover the lives of others and masquerading as something more authoritative than it is; in short, a spiritual tyranny.

There is in the condition of nature, where Christians are concerned, a law of nature; and it reposes in the scriptures. But what the commands of this law are no man can say except in regard to himself alone; the public knowledge of this law is confined to

92. *L.*, p. 224.

the knowledge of its bare existence.[93] So far, then, from the law of nature mitigating the chaos of nature, it accentuates it. To be a "natural" Christian adds a new shadow to the darkness of the predicament of the condition of nature, a shadow that will require for its removal a special provision in the deliverance.

The deliverance from the chaos of the condition of nature as hitherto conceived is by the creation of a civil association or Commonwealth; indeed, the condition of nature is the hypothetical efficient cause of a Commonwealth. And when account is taken of this new factor of chaos, the deliverance must be by the creation of a Christian Commonwealth; that is, a civil association composed of Christian subjects under a Christian sovereign authority. The creation of this requires no new covenant; the natural right of each man to interpret scripture and determine the law of God on his own behalf will be transferred with the rest of his natural right, for it is not a separable part of his general natural right. And the recipient of the transferred right is the artificial, sovereign authority, an authority which is not temporal *and* spiritual (for, "*Temporal* and *Spiritual* government are but two names brought into the world to make men see double, and mistake their lawful sovereign"),[94] but single and supreme. And the association represented in his person is not a state *and* a church, for a true church (unlike the so-called churches which pretended their claims to be independent spiritual authorities in the condition of nature) is "a company of men professing Christian Religion, united in the person of one Sovereign." It cannot be a rival spiritual authority, setting up canons against laws, a spiritual power against a civil, and determining man's conduct by eternal sanctions,[95] because there is no generation that can be imagined for such an authority and its existence would contradict the end for which society was instituted. And if the Papacy lays claim to such an authority, it can at once be pronounced a claim that any

93. *L.*, p. 275.
94. *L.*, p. 306.
95. *L.*, p. 214.

other foreign sovereign might make (for civil associations stand
in a condition of nature towards one another), only worse, for
the Pope is a sovereign without subjects, a prince without a kingdom: "if a man consider the original of this great Ecclesiastical
Dominion, he will easily perceive, that the Papacy, is no other,
than the *ghost* of the deceased *Roman Empire,* sitting crowned
on the grave thereof: For so did the Papacy, start up on a sudden
out of the ruins of that great Heathen Power."[96]

It remains to consider what it means to be a Christian sovereign and a Christian subject. The chief right of the sovereign as
Christian is the right to settle and interpret scripture and thus
determine authoritatively the rules that belong to the Law of
God and Nature. Without this right it is impossible for him to
perform the functions of his office. For, if he does not possess it,
it will be possessed either by no one (and the chaos and war of
nature will remain) or by someone else who will then, on account
of the preeminent power this right gives, wield a supremacy both
illegitimate and destructive of peace. But it is a right giving im-
mense authority, for the laws it determines may be *called* God's
laws, but are in fact the laws of the sovereign. With this right,
the sovereign will have the authority to control public worship,[97]
a control to be exercised in such a way as to oblige no subject to
do or believe anything that might endanger his eternal salvation.[98] He may suppress organized superstition and heresy,[99] because they are destructive of peace; but an inquisition into the
private beliefs of his subjects is no part of his right. And, as with
other rights of sovereignty, he may delegate his right of religious
instruction to agents whom he will choose, or even (if it be for
the good of the society) to the Pope;[100] but the authority thus
delegated is solely an authority to instruct, to give counsel and

96. *L.,* p. 457.
97. *L.,* p. 136, ch. xlii.
98. *L.,* ch. xliii.
99. *L.,* p. 453.
100. *L.,* pp. 421, 427.

advice, and not to coerce.[101] But if the sovereign as Christian has specific rights, he has also obligations. For in the Christian Commonwealth there exists a law to which the sovereign is, in a sense, obliged. What had previously been merely the rational articles of peace, have become (on being determined in scripture) obligatory rules of conduct. The sovereign, of course, has no obligations to his subjects, only functions; but the law of God is to him (though he has made it himself), no less than to his subjects, a command creating an obligation. And iniquity, which in a heathen sovereign could never be more than a failure to observe the conclusions of sound reasoning, in the Christian sovereign becomes a breach of law and therefore a sin, punishable by God.

The subject as Christian has a corresponding extension of his obligation and right. The rule of his religion, as determined by the authoritative interpretation of scripture, creates no new and independent obligations, but provides a new sanction for the observation of all his obligations. The articles of peace are for him no longer merely the conclusions of reasoning legitimately enforced by the sovereign power; they are the laws of God. To observe the covenant he has made with his fellows becomes a religious obligation as well as a piece of prudential wisdom. The freedom of the Christian subject is the silence of the law with regard to his thoughts and beliefs; for if it be the function of the sovereign to suppress controversy, he has no right to interfere with what he cannot in fact control and what if left uncontrolled will not endanger peace. "As for the inward *thought* and *belief* of men, which human governors take no notice of (for God only knoweth the heart), they are not voluntary, nor the effect of the laws, but of the unrevealed will and of the power of God; and consequently fall not under obligation."[102] It is a darkly sceptical doctrine upon which Hobbes grounds toleration.

101. *L.*, p. 384.
102. *L.*, p. 364.

The argument is finished: but let no one mistake it for the book. The skeleton of a masterpiece of philosophical writing has a power and a subtlety, but they are not to be compared with the power and subtlety of the doctrine itself, clothed in the irony and eloquence of a writer such as Hobbes.

VI. Some Topics Considered

(1) *The Criticism of Hobbes.* Most great philosophers have found some defenders who are prepared to swallow everything, even the absurdities; but Hobbes is an exception. He has aroused admiration in some of his readers, horror in others, but seldom affection and never undiscriminating affection. Nor is it surprising that this should be so. He offended against taste and interest, and his arrogance invited such a consequence. He could not deny himself the pleasure of exaggeration, and what were remembered were his incautious moments, and the rest forgotten. His doctrines, or some of them, have received serious attention and criticism from the time when they first appeared; but his critics have for the most part been opponents, and his few defenders not conspicuous for their insight into his meaning. On the whole it remains true that no great writer has suffered more at the hands of little men than Hobbes.

His opponents divide themselves into two classes; the emotional and the intellectual. Those who belong to the first are concerned with the supposed immoral tendencies of his doctrines; theirs is a practical criticism. The second are concerned with the theoretical cogency of his doctrines; they wish to shed light and sometimes succeed in doing so.

With the critics of the first class we need not greatly concern ourselves, though they still exist. They find in Hobbes nothing but an apostle of atheism, licentiousness, and despotism, and express a fitting horror at what they find. The answers to *Leviathan* constitute a library, its censors a school in themselves. Pious opinion has always been against him, and ever since he wrote he has been denounced from the pulpit. Against Hobbes, Filmer defended servitude, Harrington liberty, Clarendon the church, Locke the Englishman, Rousseau mankind, and Butler the Deity. And a writer of yesterday sums up Hobbes's reflections on civil philosophy as "the meanest of all ethical theories united with unhistorical contempt for religion to justify the most universal of absolutisms." No doubt some responsibility for all this attaches to Hobbes himself; he did not lack caution, but like all timid men he often chose the wrong occasion to be audacious. It is true that his age excused in Spinoza what it condemned in Hobbes; but then Spinoza was modest and a Jew, while Hobbes was arrogant and enough of a Christian to have known better. And that the vilification of Hobbes was not greater is due only to the fact that Machiavelli had already been cast for the part of scapegoat for the European consciousness.

The critics of the second class are more important, because it is in and through them that Hobbes has had his influence in the history of ideas. They, also, are for the most part his opponents. But, in the end, if Hobbes were alive today he would have some reason to complain (as Bradley complained) that even now he must "do most of his scepticism for himself." For his critics have shown a regrettable tendency to fix their attention on the obvious errors and difficulties and to lose sight of the philosophy as a whole. There has been a deplorable overconfidence about the exposure of faults in Hobbes's philosophy. Few accounts of it do not end with the detection of a score of simple errors, each of which is taken to be destructive of the philosophy, so that one wonders what claim Hobbes has to be a philosopher at all, let alone a great one. Of course there are inconsistencies in his doctrines, there is vagueness at critical points, there is misconception and even absurdity, and the detection of these faults is legitimate and useful criticism; but niggling of this sort will never dispose of the philosophy. A writer like Bentham may fall by his errors, but not one such as Hobbes. Nor is this the only defect of his critics. There has been failure to consider his civil philosophy in the context of the history of political philosophy, which has obscured the fact that Hobbes is not an outcast but, in purpose though not in doctrine, is an ally of Plato, Augustine, and Aquinas. There has been failure to detect the tradition to which his civil philosophy belongs, which has led to the misconception that it belongs to none and is without lineage or progeny. And a large body of criticism has been led astray by attention to superficial similarities which appear to unite Hobbes to writers with whom, in fact, he has little or nothing in common.

The task of criticism now is to make good some of these defects. It is not to be expected that it can be accomplished quickly or all at once. But a beginning may be made by reconsidering some of the vexed questions of the civil philosophy.

(2) *The Tradition of Hobbes.* Hobbes's civil philosophy is a composition based upon two themes, Will and Artifice. The individual who creates and becomes the subject of civil authority is an *ens completum,* an absolute will. He is not so much a "law unto himself" as free from all law and obligation which is the creature of law. This will is absolute because it is not conditioned or limited by any standard, rule, or rationality and has neither plan nor end to determine it. This absence of obligation is called by Hobbes, natural right. It is an original and an absolute right because it derives directly from the character of will and not from some higher law or from Reason. The proximity of several such individuals to one another is chaos. Civil association is artificial, the free creation of these absolute wills, just as nature is the free creation of the absolute will of God. It is an artifice that springs from the voluntary surrender of the unconditional freedom or right of the individual, and consequently it involves a replacement of freedom by law and right by obligation.[103] In the creation of civil association a sovereignty corresponding to the sov-

103. *L.,* ch. xxi.

ereignty of the individual is generated. The Sovereign is the product of will, and is himself representing the wills of its creators. Sovereignty is the right to make laws by willing. The Sovereign, therefore, is not himself subject to law, because law creates obligation, not right. Nor is he subject to Reason, because Reason creates nothing, neither right nor obligation. Law, the life of civil association, is the command of the Sovereign, who is the Soul (the capacity to will), not the head, of civil association.[104]

Now, two things are clear about such a doctrine. First, that its ruling ideas are those that have dominated the political philosophy of the last three hundred years. If this is Hobbes's doctrine, then Hobbes said something that allied him to the future. And secondly, it is clear that this doctrine is a breakaway from the great Rational-Natural tradition of political philosophy which springs from Plato and Aristotle and found embodiment later in the Natural Law theory. That tradition in its long history embraced and accommodated many doctrines, but this doctrine of Hobbes is something it cannot tolerate. Instead of beginning with right, it begins with law and obligation, it recognizes law as the product of Reason, it finds the only explanation of dominion in the superiority of Reason, and all the various conceptions of nature that it has entertained exclude artifice as it is conceived by Hobbes. For these reasons it is concluded that Hobbes is the originator of a new tradition in political philosophy.[105]

But this theory of Hobbes has a lineage that stretches back into the ancient world. It is true that Greek thought, lacking the conception of creative will and the idea of sovereignty, contributed a criticism of the Rational-Natural theory which fell short of the construction of an alternative tradition: Epicurus was an inspiration rather than a guide. But there are in the political ideas of Roman civilization and in the politico-theological ideas of Judaism strains of thought that carry us far outside the

104. *L.*, pp. 8, 137.
105. Strauss, *op. cit.*, ch. viii.

Rational-Natural tradition, and which may be said to constitute beginnings of a tradition of Will and Artifice. Hobbes's immediate predecessors built upon the Roman conception of *lex* and the Judaic-Christian conception of will and creation, both of which contained the seeds of opposition to the Rational-Natural tradition, seeds which had already come to an early flowering in Augustine. And by the end of the middle ages this opposition had crystallized into a living tradition of its own. Hobbes was born into the world, not only of modern science, but also of medieval thought. The scepticism and the individualism, which are the foundations of his civil philosophy, were the gifts of late scholastic nominalism; the displacement of Reason in favour of will and imagination and the emancipation of passion were slowly mediated changes in European thought that had gone far before Hobbes wrote. Political philosophy is the assimilation of political experience to an experience of the world in general, and the greatness of Hobbes is not that he began a new tradition in this respect but that he constructed a political philosophy that reflected the changes in the European intellectual consciousness which had been pioneered chiefly by the theologians of the fifteenth and sixteenth centuries. *Leviathan,* like any masterpiece, is an end and a beginning; it is the flowering of the past and the seed-box of the future. Its importance is that it is the first great achievement in the long-projected attempt of European thought to reembody in a new myth the Augustinian epic of the Fall and Salvation of mankind.

(3) *The Predicament of Mankind.* In the history of political philosophy there have been two opposed conceptions of the source of the predicament of man from which civil society springs as a deliverance: one conceived the predicament to arise out of the nature of man, the other conceived it to arise out of a defect in the nature of man. Plato, who went to what he believed to be the nature of man for the ground and structure of the *polis,* is an example of the first. And Spinoza, with his insistence on the

principle that nothing in nature must be attributed to a defect of it,[106] adheres, in his different convention, to the same project of deducing civil society from "the very condition of human nature."[107] For Augustine, on the other hand, the predicament arises from a defect in human nature, from sin. Where does Hobbes stand in this respect? The widely accepted interpretation of Hobbes's view is that, for him, the predicament springs from the egoistical character of man and that therefore it is vice and depravity that create the chaos. Moreover, it is a genuinely original depravity, for the Fall of man (or anything to take its place) is no part of Hobbes's theory. But when we look closer, what was distinguished as egoism (a moral defect) turns out to be neither moral nor a defect; it is only the individuality of a creature shut up, without hope of immediate release, within the world of his own imagination. Man is, by nature, the victim of solipsism; he is an *individua substantia* distinguished by incommunicability. And when this is understood, we are in a position to accept Hobbes's own denial of a doctrine of the natural depravity of man;[108] and he appears to take his place, on this question, beside Plato and Spinoza, basing his theory on the "known natural inclinations of mankind."[109] But not without difficulty. First, the striving after power which is characteristic of the human individual may, in Hobbes's view, be evil; it is so when it is directed by Pride. And Pride is so universal a defect in human nature that it belongs to the constitutive cause of the predicament. And, if by interpreting it as illusion Hobbes deprives Pride of moral significance, it still remains a defect. And since Pride (it will be remembered) is the Augustinian interpretation of the original sin, this doctrine of Hobbes seems to approximate his view to the conception of the predicament as springing from, not nature, but defect in nature. But secondly, the predicament for

---

106. Spinoza, *Ethica*, Pars, III, Praefatio.
107. Spinoza, *Tractatus Politicus*, § 4.
108. *E.W.*, II, xvi–xvii; *L.*, pp. 97, 224, 480.
109. *L.*, p. 554.

Hobbes is actually caused, not by an internal defect in human nature, but by something that becomes a defect when a man is among men. Pride in one may inhibit felicity, but it cannot produce chaos. On this point, then, I think our conclusion must be that Hobbes's conception of the natural man (apart from his defects) is such that a predicament requiring a deliverance is created whenever man is in proximity to man, and that his doctrine of Pride and the unpermissible form of striving after power only increases the severity of the predicament.

(4) *Individualism and Absolutism.* Individualism as a gospel has drawn its inspiration from many sources, but as a reasoned theory of society it has its roots in the so-called nominalism of late medieval scholasticism, with its doctrines that the nature of a thing is its individuality, that which makes it *this* thing, and that both in God and man will is precedent to reason. Hobbes inherited this tradition of nominalism, and more than any other writer passed it on to the modern world. His civil philosophy is based, not on any vague belief in the value or sanctity of the individual man, but on a philosophy for which the world is composed of *individuae substantiae.* This philosophy, in Hobbes, avoided on the one hand atomism (the doctrine that the individual is an indestructible particle of matter) and on the other hand universalism (the doctrine that there is but one individual, the universe), and involved both Hobbes and his successors in the conception of a scale of individuals in which the individuality of sensations and images was preserved while the individuality of the man was asserted. The human being is first fully an individual, not in respect of self-consciousness, but in the activity of willing.[110] Be-

110. Briefly, it may be said that the doctrine that sprang from the reflections of medieval philosophical thinkers distinguished two elements in personality, a rational element and a substantial element. The standard definition of *persona* was that of Boëthius—"the individual substance of a rational nature." In later medieval thought this definition suffered disruption. Emphasis upon the rational element in personality resulted, finally, in the Cartesian doctrine of the primacy of cognition and of self-consciousness as the true ground of personality. While emphasis upon the substantial

tween birth and death, the self as imagination and will is an indestructible unit, whose relations with other individuals are purely
external. Individuals may be collected together, may be added,
may be substituted for one another, or made to represent one
another, but can never modify one another or compose a whole
in which their individuality is lost. Even reason is individualized,
and becomes merely the reasoning of an individual without
power or authority to oblige acceptance by others: to convince a
man is not to enjoy a common understanding with him, but to
displace his reason by yours.[111] The natural man is the stuff of
civil association which, whatever else it is, is an association that
can comprehend such individuals without destroying them. Neither before nor after the establishment of civil association is
there any such thing as the *People,* to whom so much previous
theory ascribed sovereignty. Whatever community exists must be
generated by individual acts of will directed upon a single object,
that is, by agreement: the essence of agreement is, not a common will (for there can be no such thing), but a common object
of will. And, since these individual wills are in natural opposition
to one another, the agreement out of which *civitas* can spring
must be an agreement not to oppose one another, a will not to
will. But something more is required; merely to agree not to will
is race suicide. The agreement must be for each to transfer his
right of willing in some specific respect, to a single artificial Representative, who is thenceforth authorized to will and to act in
place of each individual. There is in this association no concord
of wills, no common will, no common good; its unity lies solely
in the singleness of the Representative, in the *substitution* of his
one will for the many conflicting wills.[112] It is a collection of indi-

element made the most of the opposition between personality and rationality and
resulted in what may be called the romantic doctrine of personality with its assertion
of the primacy of will—the person is that which is separate, incommunicable, eccentric, or even irrational. This second emphasis was the work of the late medieval nomi-
nalists, and it is the emphasis that is dominant in Hobbes.

111. *L.,* p. 33.
112. *L.,* pp. 126, 167.

viduals united in one Sovereign Representative, and in generation and structure it is the only sort of association that does not
compromise the individuality of its components.

Now, the common view is that though Hobbes may be an individualist at the beginning, his theory of civil association is designed precisely to destroy individualism. So far as the generation of civil association is concerned, this is certainly not true. To
authorize a representative to make a choice for me does not destroy or compromise my individuality; there is no confusion of
wills, so long as it is understood that my will is in the authorization of the representative and that the choice he makes is not
mine, but his on my behalf. Hobbes's individualism is far too
strong to allow even the briefest appearance of anything like a
general will.[113]

Nor is the effect generated, the Leviathan, a designed destruction of the individual; it is, in fact, the *minimum* condition
of any settled association among individuals. The Sovereign is
absolute in two respects only, and neither of them is destructive
of individuality: first, the surrender of natural right to him is absolute and his authorization is permanent and exclusive; and secondly, there is no appeal from the legitimacy of his command.
The natural right surrendered is the unconditional right, on all
occasions, to exercise one's individual will in the pursuit of felicity.[114] Now, an absolute right, if it is surrendered at all, is necessarily surrendered absolutely: Hobbes refused the compromise
which suggests that a part of the right had to be sacrificed, not
because he was an absolutist in government, but because he
knew a little elementary logic. But to surrender an absolute right
to do something on all occasions, is not to give up the right of
doing it on any occasion. For the rest, Hobbes conceives the Sovereign as a law-maker and his rule, not arbitrary, but the rule of
law. And we have already seen that law as the command of the

113. Thus, Hobbes does not say that the criminal *wills* his own punishment, but
that he is the *author* of his own punishment. *L.,* p. 167.
114. *L.,* p. 99.

Sovereign holds within itself a freedom absent from law as Reason or custom: it is Reason, not Authority, that is destructive of individuality. And, of course, the silence of the law is a further freedom; when the law does not speak the individual is sovereign over himself.[115] What, indeed, is excluded from Hobbes's *civitas* is not the freedom of the individual, but the independent rights of spurious "authorities" and of collections of individuals such as churches, which he saw as the source of the civil strife of his time.

It may be said, then, that Hobbes is not an absolutist precisely because he is an authoritarian. His scepticism about the power of reasoning, which applied no less to the "artificial reason" of the Sovereign than to the reasoning of the natural man, together with the rest of his individualism, separate him from the rationalist dictators of his or any age. Indeed, Hobbes, without being himself a liberal, had in him more of the philosophy of liberalism than most of its professed defenders.[116] He perceived the folly of his age to lie in the distraction of mankind between those who claimed too much for Authority and those who claimed too much for Liberty. The perverse authoritarians were those who forgot, or never understood, that a moral authority derives solely from an act of will of him who is obliged, and that, since the need for authority springs from the passions of men, the authority itself must be commensurate with what it has to remedy, and who therefore claimed a ground for authority outside the wills and desperate needs of mortal men. The perverse libertarians were those whose illusions led them to cling to a natural right in religion which was destructive of all that was achieved by the

---

115. *L.*, p. 163; cf. Aristotle, *Nic. Eth.*, V, xi, 1.

116. Hobbes stood in contrast to both the rationalist and the "social instinct" ethics of his contemporaries, and was attacked by representatives of both these schools. The rationalists nurtured the doctrines of antiliberalism. And it was Richard Cumberland with his "social instinct" and later Adam Smith with his "social passions" who bewitched liberalism by appearing to solve the problem of individualism when they had really only avoided it.

surrender of the rest of natural right.[117] *Autres temps, autres fo-lies:* if Hobbes were living today he would find the universal pre-dicament appearing in different particulars.

(5) *The Theory of Obligation.* Under the influence of distinctions we are now accustomed to make in discussing questions of moral theory, modern critics of Hobbes have often made the mistake of looking for an order and coherence in his thoughts on these questions which is foreign to the ideas of any seventeenth-century writer. Setting out with false expectations, we have been exasperated by the ambiguity with which Hobbes uses certain important words (such as obligation, power, duty, forbid, com-mand), and have gone on, in an attempt to understand his theory better than he understood it himself, to interpret it by *extracting* from his writings at least some consistent doctrine. This, I think, is the error that lies in attributing to him a theory of civil obliga-tion in terms of self-interest, which is an error, not because such a theory cannot be extracted from his writings, but because it gives them a simple formality which nobody supposes them to possess. Even if we confine ourselves to *Leviathan,* we are often met with obscurity and ambiguity; but Hobbes is a writer who encourages the expectation of consistency, and the most satisfac-tory interpretation will be that which gives as coherent a view as is consistent with all of what Hobbes actually wrote.

Hobbes begins with the natural right of each man to all things. Now, this right is always at least as great as a man's power to enjoy it; for, when power is sufficient a man acts,[118] and nothing that a man does can exceed what he has a natural right to do. It follows that power and natural right are equal to one another only when the power is irresistible.[119] This is so with God, in whom right and power are equal because his power is as absolute

---

117. *L.*, p. 337; *E.W.*, VI, 190.
118. *E.W.*, I, 128. Power is another name for cause, act for effect.
119. *Elements of Law*, p. 56.

as his right.[120] But it is not so with men; for, in the unavoidable competition, a man's power, so far from being irresistible, is merely equal to the power of any other man. Indeed, his natural right, which is absolute, must be vastly greater than his power which, in the circumstances, is small because it is uncertain. It appears, then, that while natural right is absolute, power is a variable quality. Natural right and the power to enjoy it are, therefore, two different considerations; neither is the cause of the other, and even where (as in God) they are equal, they are still not identifiable with one another. Might and Right are never the same thing.

According to Hobbes, for a man to be "obliged" is for him to be bound, to be constrained by some external impediment imposed, directly or indirectly, by himself. It is to suffer some specific self-inflicted diminution of his freedom which may be in respect of his right to act or of both his right and his power to act. And in this connection to do and not to do are alike to act.

First, then, were a man to be constrained from willing and performing a certain action because he judged its likely consequences to be damaging to himself, he would suffer no external constraint and therefore could not properly be said to be "obliged" to refrain from this action. Here the so-called constraint is internal, a combination of rational judgement and fear, which is aversion from something believed to be hurtful. Neither his right to do what he wills to do nor his power to do it have suffered any qualification: he remains "governed by his own reason." Thus, no man may be said to be "obliged" to act rationally so long as rationality is understood in terms of theorems about the likely consequences of actions; and fear, even if it is fear of being thwarted by the power of another man, is, as we have seen, a reason for acting or refraining from a particular action, not an external constraint upon conduct. Secondly, were a man to will to perform an action which he is unable to perform from his own

120. *L.*, p. 276.

lack of power to do so (e.g. to lift a weight beyond his capacity to lift), he could not properly be said to be "obliged" to refrain from the action. He is deprived of nothing: his right to will remains intact and he never had the power he lacks. And thirdly, a man prevented by the power (and not merely the fear of the power) of another from performing an action he has willed and is otherwise able to perform, or one compelled by another to move in a manner he has not chosen to move, is certainly constrained, and his freedom is in some specific respect diminished. But here the constraint is solely in respect of this power; it leaves unimpaired his right to do as he wills. He is deprived of one of the qualities of a free man, the exercise of his ability to do as he wishes. But, although the constraint here is certainly external and although his freedom is substantially diminished, this constraint and this diminution are not self-imposed and consequently he cannot properly be said to be "obliged" to do what he is compelled to do or to desist from what he is prevented from doing.

In order to be obliged, then, or (avoiding the confusion of common speech) in order to have an obligation, a man must himself perform an action which obligates him: there is, strictly speaking, "no obligation on any man, which ariseth not from some act of his own."[121] This act must be one which acknowledges or imposes constraint upon his unconditional right to do whatever he wills and has power to do, thus diminishing his natural freedom. The constraint imposed or acknowledged must be limited and specific: to surrender his right completely would be to obliterate himself and there would be nothing left to be obligated. That is, the act must be a surrender not of the right but of the unconditionality of the right. Further, if (as it must be) this constraint is to be external it cannot arise from merely putting-by the unconditionality of the right; it must be the giving up of whatever is given up to another who then has the right to enjoy

121. *L.*, p. 166.

it. And lastly, an obligation undertaken cannot lapse merely by a failure to fulfil it; it can be ended only in an agreement that it shall be terminated or (if it is temporary) in reaching its natural terminus—a promise fulfilled.

Now, since to undertake an obligation is always to perform a voluntary act of self-denial, it must always be done in the hope of acquiring some benefit. No man can voluntarily "despoil" himself of any part of his unconditional right knowing that it will be to his disadvantage. And the only "good" any man can recognize is the satisfaction of his wants and the avoidance of that greatest of all dissatisfactions, death. It is to this end that men bind themselves, undertake duties and become capable of injustice or injury to others which are the outcomes of not observing obligations. Thus, they make promises to one another and enter into agreement of mutual trust, designing thereby to make more secure the satisfaction of their wants. These obligations are genuine; they are voluntary undertakings which, on that account, *ought* not to be made void by those who undertake them. Nevertheless, the situation of one who accepts a promise or one who is the first performer in an agreement of mutual trust remains hazardous, for the *strength* of the bonds of obligation lies not in themselves but in the fear of the evil consequences of breaking them. And, in the circumstances, these evil consequences are nothing more than what lies within the power of the party bilked to impose and the fear of them is, therefore, not notably compelling.

But there is a way in which human beings may acquire less transitory obligations, although these also are the outcome of voluntary actions. If the theorems of natural reason about prudent conduct (theorems such as "honesty is, on the whole, the best policy") were to be recognized as the *laws* of a God, and if further this God were to be recognized as their God and they to lie within the jurisdiction of these rules, they would have acknowledged their conduct to be subject to these rules and would have obligated themselves to observe them. In this situation they

are alike bound by a known external impediment to the exercise
of their unconditional right to do what each wills and has power
to do. In a voluntary act of acknowledgement they would have
submitted themselves to the rule of divine commands. They
have not authorized God to make rules for their guidance and
they have not endowed him with power to enforce these rules,
but they know that he exists, that he is a law-giver and omnipotent, and they have acknowledged themselves to be his Subjects.
Henceforth the reason why, for example, they *ought* to keep the
agreements they have undertaken is not merely that they ought
not "to make void voluntary acts of their own" but that God has
ruled that agreements made ought to be kept. And the advantage they hope to gain from this acknowledgement is the benefit
of the approval of the ruler of the universe and perhaps also "reward in heaven" for obeying his commands. What they have
handed over in this acknowledgement is the right of each to rule
himself according to his own natural reason. But they remain
free to disobey these divine laws and, so far as life on earth is
concerned, with a fair chance of impunity. This God is omnipotent, but he has no agents on earth equipped with power to enforce penalties for disobedience. This obligation, and transitory
obligations such as those which arise from making promises to
private persons, may be said to be examples of pure but imperfect "moral" obligation. Nothing is given up save the right of a
man to govern his own conduct; nothing is provided save a bare
rule of conduct.

What, then, is *civil* obligation? Like all other obligations, it
arises from a voluntary act. This act is a notional covenant between many in which the right of each to govern himself by his
own reason is surrendered and a sovereign Actor (the occupant
of an artificially created office) is authorized to exercise it on
their behalf; that is, to declare, to interpret, and to administer
rules of conduct which the covenanters pledge themselves in advance to obey. The persons concerned are under no obligation
to make any such agreement among themselves; they are merely

instructed to do so by reason and fear. Thus, civil obligation is a "moral" obligation; it arises from a genuine surrender of *right*. Furthermore, it comprehends all other moral obligation. It is true that the subjects of a civil sovereign may have acknowledged themselves to be obligated to the laws of a God known to them by their natural reason and even to one whose will is also revealed in prophetic utterances (scripture). But first, a civil subject cannot know where his duty lies if he understands himself to be obligated by two possibly divergent sets of laws; and secondly, God has not himself provided an authoritative apparatus (a court of law) for deciding the meaning of his laws in contingent circumstances, and while this is so the obligations they entail remain imperfectly specified; what they mean is almost anybody's guess. Consequently, on both these counts, it falls to the civil sovereign to specify his subjects' obligations; he must assimilate divine to civil law and he must provide an official interpretation of the meaning in contingent circumstances of all the rules which govern his subjects' conduct. And there is something more which distinguishes civil obligation. In addition to binding themselves each to surrender his right to govern himself, the covenanters who thus create a *civitas* pledge themselves to use all their strength and power on behalf of the civil sovereign; that is, they obligate themselves not only in respect of their right to govern themselves, but in respect also of the use of their power. This, then, is the unique characteristic and special virtue of civil obligation and civil association: a subject obligated both in respect of his right to act and his power to act, and an association equipped with known and authoritative rules of conduct which cannot be breached with impunity.

(6) *Civil Theology.* Long before the time of Hobbes the severance of religion from civil life, which was one of the effects of early Christianity, had been repealed. But the significant change observable in the seventeenth century was the appearance of states in which religion and civil life were assimilated to one an-

other as closely as the universalist tradition of Christianity would permit. It was a situation reminiscent at least of the ancient world, where religion was a communal *cultus* of communal deities. In England, Hooker had theorized this assimilation in the style of a medieval theologian; it was left to Hobbes to return to a more ancient theological tradition (indeed, a pagan tradition) and to theorize it in a more radical fashion.

In the later middle ages it had become customary to divide Theology, the doctrine concerning divine things, into a part concerned with what is accessible by the light of natural reason (and here the doctrine was largely Aristotelian in inspiration), and a part concerned with what is known only through the revelation of scripture. Theology, that is, was both Rational and Revealed. This way of thinking had sprung, by a long process of mediation, from the somewhat different view of the *genera theologiae* that belonged to the late Roman world for which the contrast was between Rational Theology (again largely derived from Aristotle) and Civil Theology.[122] This last was the consideration of the doctrines and beliefs of religions actually practised in civil communities. It was not concerned with philosophic speculation or proof, with first causes or the existence of God, but solely with the popular beliefs involved in a religious *cultus*. It is to this tradition that Hobbes returned. Of course, the immediate background of his thought was the political theology of the late middle ages and the Reformation; and, of course, scripture was the authoritative source to which he went to collect the religious beliefs of his society. And it is not to be supposed that he made any conscious return to an earlier tradition, or that his way of thinking was unique in his generation. What is suggested is that he has more in common with the secular theologians of the Italian Renaissance than with a writer such as Erastus, and that he treats the religion of his society as he finds it in the scriptures,

---

122. Augustine, *De Civitate Dei,* Bk. VI.

not in the style of a Protestant theologian, but rather in the style of Varro.

Hobbes's doctrine runs something like this. Religious belief is something not to be avoided in this world, and is something of the greatest practical importance. Its generation is from fear arising out of the unavoidable limits of human experience and reasoning. There can be no "natural knowledge of man's estate after death,"[123] and consequently there can be no natural religion in the accepted meaning of the term. Natural religion implies a universal natural Reason; but not only is reasoning confined to what may be concluded from the utterances of the senses, but it is never more than the reasoning of some individual man. There is, then, first, the universal and necessary lack of knowledge of things beyond the reach of sense; secondly, innumerable particular expressions of this lack of knowledge in the religious fears of human beings; and thirdly, the published collection in the Christian scriptures of the fears of certain individuals, which has become the basis of the religious idiom of European civilization. And the result is confusion and strife; confusion because the scriptures are at the mercy of each man's interpretation, strife because each man is concerned to force his own fears on other men or on account of them to claim for himself a unique way of living.

To those of Hobbes's contemporaries for whom the authority of medieval Christianity was dead, there appeared to be two possible ways out of this chaos of religious belief. There was first the way of natural religion. It was conceived possible that, by the light of natural Reason, a religion, based upon "the unmoveable foundations of truth,"[124] and supplanting the inferior religions of history, might be found in the human heart, and receiving universal recognition, become established among mankind. Though

123. *L.,* p. 113.
124. Herbert of Cherbury, *De Veritate,* p. 117.

their inspiration was older than Descartes, those who took this way found their guide in Cartesian rationalism, which led them to the fairyland of Deism and the other fantasies of the *saeculum rationalisticum,* amid the dim ruins of which we now live. The other way was that of a civil religion, not the construction of reason but of authority, concerned not with belief but with practice, aiming not at undeniable truth but at peace. Such a religion was the counterpart of the sovereign civil association. And civil philosophy, in its project of giving this civil association an intellectual foundation, could not avoid the responsibility of constructing a civil theology, the task of which was to find in the complexities of Christian doctrine a religion that could be an authorized public religion, banishing from civil association the confusion and strife that came from religious division. This was the way of Hobbes. He was not a natural theologian; the preconceptions of natural theology and natural religion were foreign to his whole philosophy; he was a civil theologian of the old style but in new circumstances. For him, religion was actual religious beliefs, was Christianity. He was not concerned to reform those beliefs in the interest of some universal, rational truth about God and the world to come, but to remove from them the power to disrupt society. The religion of the seventeenth century was, no less than the religion of any other age, a religion in which fear was a major constituent. And Hobbes, no less than others of his time—Montaigne and Pascal, for example—felt the impact of this fear; he died in mortal fear of hell-fire. But whereas in an earlier age Lucretius conceived the project of releasing men from the dark fears of their religion by giving them the true knowledge of the gods, no such project could enter the mind of Hobbes. That release, for him, could not come from any knowledge of the natural world; if it came at all it must be the work of time, not reason. But meanwhile it was the less imposing task of civil theology to make of that religion something not inimical to civilized life.

(7) *Beyond Civility.* Political philosophy, I have suggested, is the consideration of the relation between civil association and eternity. The *civitas* is conceived as the deliverance of a man observed to stand in need of deliverance. This, at least, is the ruling idea of many of the masterpieces of political philosophy, *Leviathan* among them. In the Preface to the Latin edition Hobbes says: "This great Leviathan, which is called the State, is a work of art; it is an artificial man made for the protection and salvation of the natural man, to whom it is superior in grandeur and power." We may, then, enquire of any political philosophy conceived on this plan, whether the gift of civil association to mankind is, in principle, the gift of salvation itself, or whether it is something less, and if the latter, what relation it bears to salvation. The answers to these questions will certainly tell us something we should know about a political philosophy; indeed, they will do more, they will help us to determine its value.

When we turn to make this enquiry of the great political philosophies, we find that, each in its own convention, they maintain the view that civil association is contributory to the fulfilment of an end which it cannot itself bring about; that the achievement in civil association is a tangible good and not, therefore, to be separated from the deliverance that constitutes the whole good, but something less than the deliverance itself. For both Plato and Aristotle civil association is not man's highest activity, and what is achieved in it must always fall short of the best life, which is a contemplative, intellectual life. And the contribution of the *civitas* to the achievement of this end is the organization of human affairs so that no one who is able may be prevented from enjoying it.[125] For Augustine the *justitia* and *pax* that are the gifts of civil association are no more than the necessary remedy for the immediate consequences of the original sin; they have a specific relation to the justice of God and the *pax coelestis,* but they

125. Plato, *Republic,* 614 *sq.*; Aristotle, *Nic. Eth.,* X, vii–ix.

cannot themselves bring about that "perfectly ordered union of hearts in the enjoyment of God and one another in God."[126] For Aquinas a *communitas politica* may give to man a natural happiness, but this, while it is related to the supernatural happiness, is not itself more than a secondary deliverance from evil in the eternal life of the soul. And Spinoza, who perhaps more completely than any other writer adheres to the conception of human life as a predicament from which salvation is sought, finds in civil association no more than a second-best deliverance, giving a freedom that cannot easily be dispensed with, but one not to be compared with that which belongs to him who is delivered from the power of necessity by his knowledge of the necessary workings of the universe.[127]

Now, in this matter Hobbes is perhaps more suspect than any other great writer. This alleged apostle of absolutism would, more than others, appear to be in danger of making civil association a hell by conceiving it as a heaven. And yet there is little justification for the suspicion. For Hobbes, the salvation of man, the true resolution of his predicament, is neither religious nor intellectual, but emotional. Man above all things else is a creature of passion, and his salvation lies, not in the denial of his character, but in its fulfilment. And this is to be found, not in pleasure—those who see in Hobbes a hedonist are sadly wide of the mark—but in Felicity, a transitory perfection, having no finality and offering no repose. Man, as Hobbes sees him, is not engaged in an undignified scramble for suburban pleasures; there is the greatness of great passion in his constitution. The restless desire that moves him is not pain,[128] nor may it be calmed by any momentary or final achievement;[129] and what life in another world has to offer, if it is something other than Felic-

126. Augustine, *De Civitate Dei*, xix, 13.
127. Spinoza, *Ethica*, Pars, V.
128. Locke, *Human Understanding*, II, xxi, 32.
129. Aquinas, *Summa Theologica*, II, i, 1. Q. 27. 1.

ity, is a salvation that has no application to the man we know.[130] For such a man salvation is difficult; indeed what distinguishes Hobbes from all earlier and most later writers is his premise that a man is a moving "body," that human conduct is inertial, not teleological movement, and that his "salvation" lies in "continual success in obtaining those things which a man from time to time desires." And certainly civil association has no power to bring this about. Nevertheless, what it offers is something of value relative to his salvation. It offers the removal of some of the circumstances that, if they are not removed, must frustrate the enjoyment of Felicity. It is a negative gift, merely making not impossible that which is sought. Here, in civil association, is neither fulfilment nor wisdom to discern fulfilment, but peace, the only condition of human life that can be permanently established. And to a race condemned to seek its perfection in the flying moment and always in the one to come, whose highest virtue is to cultivate a clear-sighted vision of the consequences of its actions, and whose greatest need (not supplied by nature) is freedom from the distraction of illusion, the Leviathan, that *justitiae mensura atque ambitionis elenchus*, will appear an invention neither to be despised nor overrated. "When the springs dry up, the fish are all together on dry land. They will moisten each other with their dampness and keep each other wet with their slime. But this is not to be compared with their forgetting each other in a river or a lake."

1946 and 1974

130. *L.*, p. 48.

2

The Moral Life in the Writings of Thomas Hobbes

1

The moral life is a life *inter homines*. Even if we are disposed to
look for a remote ground (such, for example, as the will of God)
for our moral obligations, moral conduct concerns the relations
of human beings to one another and the power they are capable
of exerting over one another. This, no doubt, spills over into
other relationships—those with animals, for example, or even
with things—but the moral significance of these lies solely in
their reflection of the dispositions of men towards one another.
Further, the moral life appears only when human behaviour is
free from natural necessity; that is, when there are alternatives
in human conduct. It does not require that a specific choice
should be made on each occasion, for moral conduct may be
habit; it does not require that each occasion should find a man
without a disposition to behave in a certain manner; and it does
not require that on any occasion the range of choices should be
unlimited. But it does require the possibility of choice, and we
may perhaps suppose that specific choices of some sort (though
not necessarily the choice of *this* action) have been made at
some time even though they have become lost and superseded
in a settled disposition. In other words, moral conduct is art, not
nature: it is the exercise of an acquired skill. But the skill here

is not that of knowing how to get what we want with the least expenditure of energy, but knowing how to behave as we *ought* to behave: the skill, not of desiring, but of approving and of doing what is approved.

All this is, of course, well known. Every moralist has perceived a gap between the ascertained inclinations of human beings and what ought to be done about them. But there is something else to be observed, namely, that what we ought to do is unavoidably connected with what in fact we are; and what we are is (in this connection) what we believe ourselves to be. And a moralist who fails to recognize this is apt to fall into absurdity. What Hume complained of was not the attempt to ascertain the connection between moral and factual propositions but the hasty and unsatisfactory manner in which this was done. It was the acute Vauvenargues who detected that it was only by the subterfuge of inventing a "virtu incompatible avec la natur de l'homme" that La Rochefoucauld was able to announce coldly that "il n'y avait aucun virtu." Indeed, the idioms of moral conduct which our civilization has displayed are distinguished, in the first place, not in respect of their doctrines about how we *ought* to behave, but in respect of their interpretations of what in fact we are.

There are, I believe, three such idioms, which I shall denote: first, the morality of communal ties; secondly, the morality of individuality; and thirdly, the morality of the common good.

In the morality of communal ties, human beings are recognized solely as members of a community and all activity whatsoever is understood to be communal activity. Here, separate individuals, capable of making choices for themselves and inclined to do so, are unknown, not because they have been suppressed but because the circumstances in which they might have appeared are absent. And here, good conduct is understood as appropriate participation in the unvarying activities of a community. It is as if all the choices had already been made and what ought to be done appears, not in general rules of conduct, but in a detailed ritual from which divergence is so difficult that there seems to be no visible alternative to it. What ought to be done is indistinguishable from what is done; art appears as nature. Nevertheless, this is an idiom of *moral* conduct, because the manner of this communal activity is, in fact, art and not nature; it is the product, not (of course) of design, but of numberless, long-forgotten choices.

In the morality of individuality, on the other hand, human beings are recognized (because they have come to recognize themselves in this character) as separate and sovereign individuals, associated with one another, not in the pursuit of a single common enterprise, but in an enterprise of give and take, and accommodating themselves to one another as best they can: it is the morality of self and other selves. Here individual choice is preeminent and a great part of happiness is connected with its exercise. Moral conduct is recognized as consisting in determinate relationships between these individuals, and the conduct approved is that which reflects the independent individuality understood to be characteristic of human beings. Morality is the art of mutual accommodation.

The morality of the common good springs from a different reading of human nature, or (what is the same thing) the emergence of a different idiom of human character. Human beings are recognized as independent centres of activity, but approval attaches itself to conduct in which this individuality is suppressed whenever it conflicts, not with the individuality of others, but with the interests of a "society" understood to be composed of such human beings. All are engaged in a single, common enterprise. Here the lion and the ox are distinguished from one another, but there is not only one *law* for both, there is a single approved condition of circumstance for both: the lion shall eat straw like the ox. This single approved condition of human circumstance is called "the social good," "the good of all," and morality is the art in which this condition is achieved and maintained.

Perhaps a deeper review of the history of European morals

would disclose other general moral dispositions to be added to these, and perhaps my descriptions of those I have noticed are unnaturally precise, ideal extrapolations of what has actually been felt; but I have no doubt that dispositions of these kinds have appeared, and (without ever quite superseding one another) they have followed one another during the last thousand years of our history, each in turn provoking moral reflection appropriate to itself.

2

In considering the writings of a moralist the first thing to be ascertained is, then, the understanding he has of the nature of human beings. And in Hobbes we may recognize a writer who was engaged in exploring that idiom of the moral life I have called the morality of individuality. Nor is it at all remarkable that this should be so. It is only a very poor moralist who invents for himself either virtues or a version of human nature; both precepts and his reading of human character he must take from the world around him. And, since the emergent human character of western Europe in the seventeenth century was one in which a feeling for individuality was becoming preeminent—the independent, enterprising man out to seek his intellectual or material fortune, and the individual human soul responsible for its own destiny—this unavoidably became for Hobbes, as it was for his contemporary moralists, the subject matter of moral reflection. For Hobbes (or for any other moralist in the seventeenth and eighteenth centuries) to have undertaken to explore either the morality of communal ties or the morality of the common good would have been an anachronism. What, then, distinguishes Hobbes from his contemporaries is not the idiom of the moral life he chose to explore, but the precise manner in which he interpreted this current sentiment for individuality and the doctrine of moral conduct he associated with it, or purported to deduce from it. And if it is the enterprise of every philosopher to translate current sentiments into the idiom of general ideas and to universalize a local version of human character by finding for it some rational ground, this enterprise was fortified in Hobbes by his notion of philosophy as the science of deducing the general causes of observed occurrences. His concern was with both men and things; but he was content to allow a certain looseness in the connection between the two,[1] and unlike Spinoza, who presents us with a universe composed of metaphysical individualities (man being only a special case of a universal condition), Hobbes's starting-point as a moralist was with unique *human* individuality; and, as he understood it, his first business was to rationalize *this* individuality by displaying its "cause," its components and its structure.

Hobbes's complex image of human character was settled upon what he calls "two most certain postulates of human nature," namely, the postulate of "natural appetite" or passion, and the postulate of "natural reason."[2] It was an image which, in various idioms, had haunted European reflection for many centuries, and though its most familiar idiom is Christian, it is traceable in the Latin thought of pagan antiquity. It is displayed in the lines of the sixteenth-century poet Fulke Greville:

> O wearisome condition of humanity,
> Born to one law and to another bound,
> Vainly begot and yet forbidden vanity,
> Created sick, commanded to be sound,
> What meaneth nature by these diverse laws,
> Passion and Reason, self-division's cause.

But, whereas the poet is content to compose an image, the philosopher's task is to resolve its incoherence and to make it intelligible.

1. *E.W.*, II, xx.
2. *E.W.*, II, vii.

Any abridgement of Hobbes's carefully pondered and exceedingly complicated image of human nature is hazardous, but to follow all its intricacies is impossible now. To be brief—at least as compared with Hobbes himself—he understood a human being to be a bodily structure characterized by internal movements. There is, first, what he called *vital* movement, the involuntary movement which is identified with being alive and which is exemplified in the circulation of the blood and in breathing. This bodily structure, however, exists in an environment to which it is sensitive, and its contacts with this environment are felt either to assist its vital movements or to impede them. Experiences friendly to vital movement are pleasures and are recognized as good; those which are hostile to it are pains and recognized as evil. Thus, pleasure and pain are our own introspective awareness of being alive; and we prefer pleasure to pain because we prefer life to death. Further, what we prefer we endeavour to bring about. We endeavour to experience those contacts which promote our vital movements and to avoid those which hinder them; and these endeavours are understood by Hobbes as incipient movements towards and away from the components of our environment, movements which he calls respectively appetites and aversions.

In general, for Hobbes, this account of being alive applied both to human beings and to animals, and some of it, perhaps, to other organisms also: an original endowment of vital movement stimulated or hindered by contacts with an environment, and a primordial aversion from death. But at this point Hobbes distinguished between human beings and other organisms. An animal, for example, may feel pleasure and pain, but its vital movements are affected only by an environment with which it is in immediate contact, its appetites and aversions are movements of like and dislike only in relation to what is present, and its hunger is the hunger of the moment.[3] But human beings have other en-

3. *Leviathan*, p. 82.

dowments which amplify the range of their appetites and aversions. The chief of these are memory and imagination. Human beings are capable of storing up their experiences of pleasure and pain and of recollecting their causes at a later time; and, in addition to their inescapable environment of objects, they surround themselves with a world of imagined experiences, and they are capable of desiring what is not present except in imagination. Their appetites are inventive and self-consciously pursued, and they are capable of voluntary movements for the achievement of their imagined ends and not merely of reflex responses to whatever happens to constitute their environment. To the simple passions of desire and love, of aversion and hate and of joy and grief, are added hope and despair, courage and anger, ambition, repentance, covetousness, jealousy, and revenge. They desire not only an environment presently favourable to their vital movements, but a command over that environment which will ensure its friendliness in the future; and the end they seek, Felicity, is not, properly speaking, an end, but merely "continual success in obtaining those things which a man from time to time desireth."[4] They are, however, restless and ever unsatisfied, not merely because the world is continually provoking them to fresh responses, but because the appetite of an imaginative creature is essentially unsatisfiable. They have "a restless desire for power after power which ceaseth only in death," not because they are driven to seek ever "more intensive delights," but because they cannot be assured of the power to live well which they have at present without the acquisition of more.

Moreover, as Hobbes understood it, although men and animals are alike in their self-centredness, the characteristic difference between them lies in the competitive nature of human appetite and passion: every man wishes to outdo all other men. "Man, whose Joy consisteth in comparing himself with other

4. *L.*, p. 48.

men, can relish nothing but what is eminent."[5] Human life, consequently, is a race which has "no other goal, nor other garland, but being foremost"; Felicity is "continually to outgo the next before."[6] Indeed, the greatest pleasure of a human being, what most of all stimulates the vital movement of his heart, is the consciousness of his own power; the spring of his natural appetite is not what the present world offers him, but his desire for precedence, his longing to be first, for glory and to be recognized and honoured[7] by other men as preeminent. His supreme and characteristic passion is Pride; he wishes above all else to be convinced of his own superiority. And so strong is this desire that he is apt to try to satisfy it in make-believe, if (as is usually the case) actual circumstances deny it to him. Thus, pride may degenerate into vainglory, (the mere supposition of glory "for delight in the consequences of it"); and in the illusions of vainglory he loses ground in the race for precedence.[8]

The passion of pride has, however, a partner; namely, fear. In animals, fear may be understood as merely being affrighted, but in man it is something much more important. Any creature of imagination engaged in maintaining his superiority over others of his kind must be apprehensive of not being able to do so. Fear, here, is not merely being anxious lest the next pleasure escape him, but dread of falling behind in the race and thus being denied felicity. And every such dread is a reflection of the ultimate fear, the fear of death. But, whereas animals may fear anything which provokes aversion, with men the chief fear (before which all others are of little account) is fear of the other competitors in the race. And whereas with animals the ultimate dread is death in any manner, the ultimate fear in man is the dread of violent

5. *L.*, p. 130.
6. *Elements of Law*, I, ix, 21.
7. To "honour" a man is to esteem him to be of great power. *E.W.*, IV, 257.
8. *Elements*, I, ix, 1; *L.*, pp. 44, 77.

(or untimely)[9] death at the hand of another man; for this is dishonour, the emblem of all *human* failure. This is the fear which Hobbes said is the human passion "to be reckoned with": its spring is not a mere desire to remain alive in adverse circumstances, nor is it a mere aversion from death, least of all from the pain of death; its spring is aversion from shameful death.

Human life is, then, a tension between pride and fear; each of these primary passions elucidates the character of the other, and together they define the ambivalent relationship which men enjoy with one another. They need one another, for without others there is no precedence, no recognition of superiority, no honour, no praise, no notable felicity; nevertheless every man is the enemy of every man and is engaged in a competition for superiority in which he is unavoidably apprehensive of failure.[10]

So much, then, for the postulate of "natural appetite" and its entailments in human disposition and conduct. But there is a second postulate, that of "natural reason."

"Reason," "rational," and "reasoning" are words which, in Hobbes's vocabulary, signify various human powers, endowments, and aptitudes which, though they are related to one another, are not identical. In general, they are words which stand for powers which distinguish men, not from one another, but from animals. Human beings are different from beasts in respect of having two powers which may be recognized as, at least, intimations of rationality. First, they are able to regulate their

---

9. *L.*, p. 100.

10. This is the "warre of every man, against every man" (*L.*, p. 96), understood by Hobbes to be a permanent condition of universal hostility. It is, of course, a mistake to suppose that Hobbes invented this image of "natural" human relations (it goes back at least to Augustine, who took the story of Cain and Abel to be the emblem of it), what he did was to rationalize it in a new manner, detaching it from "sin." Further, Hobbes distinguished this condition from another, also called "warre," where hostility is both intermittent and particular and which he recognized as a means by which a condition of peace (a *civitas*) might be established and defended, which the "warre of every man against every man" could never be.

"Traynes of Thoughts" in such a manner as, not merely to perceive the cause of what has been imagined, but, "when imagining any thing whatsoever, [to] seek all the possible effects, that can be produced by it; that is to say, [to] imagine what [they] can do with it, when [they] have it."[11] In other words, human processes of thinking have a scope and an orderliness denied to those of beasts because in them sensation is supplemented by reasoning. This, it seems, is a natural endowment. Secondly, human beings have the power of Speech;[12] and speech is the transference of the "Trayne of our Thoughts into a Trayne of Words."[13] This power is a special endowment received from God ("the first author of Speech") by Adam when he was taught by God how to name such creatures as were presented to his sight; and it is the condition of that uniquely human power of "reasoning," the power of putting words together in a significant manner and of composing arguments. Nevertheless, the power of Speech has to be learned afresh by each generation, and a child becomes recognizable as a "Reasonable Creature" only when it has "attained the use of Speech."[14]

The first use of words is as "*Markes, or Notes* of remembrance" and to register the consequences of our thoughts.[15] But they may be used also to communicate with other men; to communicate both information and desires. Beasts, it is true, have some means of communicating their desires to one another; but, not having the use of words, they are unable to communicate (what, because of the narrowness of their imaginations, they have not got), namely, those long-term, considered enterprises which in human beings are properly called "wills and purposes." Their power of communication, and consequently the agree-

---

11. *L.*, p. 20.
12. *L.*, ch. iv.
13. *L.*, p. 24.
14. *L.*, p. 37.
15. *L.*, p. 25.

ment they may have with one another, is "natural" or instinctive.[16] Among men, on the other hand, communication is by means of the artifice of words. By these means they can (among much else) "make known to others [their] wills and purposes, that [they] may have the mutual help of one another."[17] Speech, then, is the ground of such mutual understanding as human beings enjoy among themselves; and this mutual understanding is the ground of any agreement they may have with one another in the pursuit of their desires. Indeed, as Hobbes understands it, Speech itself (as a means of communication) is based upon agreement—agreement about the significance of words.

Generally speaking, agreement between human beings appears only in specific agreements, and these may be of three different sorts. Sometimes it happens that a man, wanting what another man has and is willing to part with if he is recompensed, an exchange may be agreed upon and concluded on the spot, as with buying and selling with ready money. This is a situation described by Hobbes as one in which the thing and the right to the thing are transferred together.[18] And however mistrustful one may be of the man with whom one makes such a bargain, the only disappointment one may suffer is the disappointment to which every buyer is liable, namely, finding that what he has bought turns out to be different from what he had expected it to be. On other occasions, however, the right may be transferred before the thing itself is handed over, as when for a sum of money paid an undertaking is given to deliver tomorrow what has been purchased, or when a man agrees to do a week's work for payment to be received at the end of the week. Such an agreement is called a Pact or Covenant, one party promising and the other performing and waiting for the promise to be fulfilled. In other words, Covenant is an agreement entailing credit. And this element of credit is supremely characteristic of the third

16. *L.*, pp. 130 *sq.*
17. *L.*, p. 25.
18. *L.*, p. 102.

kind of agreement; what Hobbes calls "covenants of mutual trust." These are Covenants in which neither party "presently performs," but both agree to perform later. And it is in respect of these that "reason" gives its most unmistakable warning and in which the true predicament of men in a state of nature is revealed.

Human beings, then, on account of the scope of their imaginations (embracing the future as well as the present), and on account of their powers of speech, are recognizable as contract-and-covenant-making creatures: their agreement is not "natural" but executed in "artificial" agreements.[19] Moreover, since agreements may be recognized as endeavours to modify the condition of suspicion and hostility which is their natural circumstance, and therefore to modify the fear that this condition entails, human beings have, in general, a sufficient motive for entering into them. But the regrettable fact is that the relief given by this otherwise most useful sort of agreement (that is, Pacts or Covenants of mutual trust) is uncertain and apt to be evanescent. For in these one party must perform first, before the other keeps his part of the bargain, and the risk of him who is to be the second performer not keeping his promise (either because it may not then be in his interest to do so, or, more probably, because "ambition" and "avarice" have intervened) must always be great enough to make it unreasonable for any man to consent to be the first performer. Thus, while such covenants may be entered into reason warns us against being the first to execute them,[20] and therefore against entering into them except as second performers. In short, if "reason" merely enabled human beings to communicate and to make covenants with one another, it must be recognized as a valuable endowment but insufficient to resolve the tension between pride and fear. This, however, is not the limit of its usefulness: these "rational" powers also reveal the

19. *L.*, p. 131. Covenants, of course, are not possible between men and beasts; but they are also impossible without an intermediary with God. *L.*, p. 106.

20. *L.*, p. 131.

manner in which the defects of covenanted agreements may be remedied and make possible the emancipation of the human race from the frustrations of natural appetite.

"Reason," here, as Hobbes understood it, is not an arbitrary imposition upon the passionate nature of man; indeed, it is generated by the passion of fear itself. For fear, in human beings, is active and inventive; it provokes in them, not a mere disposition to retreat, but "a certain foresight of future evil" and the impulse to "take heed" and to provide against what is feared. "They who travel carry their swords with them, . . . and even the strongest armies, and most accomplished for fight, [yet] sometimes parley for peace, as fearing each other's power, and lest they might be overcome."[21] In short, fear of the mischances that may befall him in the race awakens man from his dreams of vainglory (for any belief in continuous superiority is an illusion) and forces upon his attention the true precariousness of his situation.

His first reaction is to triumph by disposing of his immediate enemy, the one next before him in the race for precedence; but "reason" rejects this as a short-sighted triumph—there will always remain others to be disposed of and there will always remain the uncertainty of being able to dispose of them. And besides, to dispose of an enemy is to forgo recognition of one's own superiority, that is, to forgo felicity.[22] What has to be achieved is a permanent release from fear of dishonourable death; and reason, generated by fear and pronouncing for the avoidance of the threat of death as the condition of the satisfaction of any appetite, declares for an agreed modification of the race for precedence, that is, for a condition of peace. The consequence of natural appetite is pride and fear; the "suggestion" and promise of reason is peace. And peace, the product of the mutual recognition of a common enemy (death) is to be achieved only in a condition of common subjection to an artificially created sovereign

21. *E.W.*, II, 6 fn.
22. Cf. *L.*, pp. 549–50.

authority, that is, in the *civitas*.[23] There, under a civil law made and enforced by a Common Power authorized to do so, Covenants lose their uncertainty and become "constant and lasting," and the war of every man against every man is brought to an end. The endeavour for peace is natural, begotten by human reason upon human fear; the condition of peace is a contrivance, designed (or discerned) by reason and executed in an agreement of "every man with every man" in which each surrenders his "right to govern himself" to a "common authority."[24]

To survive, then, is seen to be more desirable than to stand first; proud men must become tame men in order to remain alive. Yet, if we accept this as Hobbes's solution of the predicament of natural man, incoherence remains. Human life is interpreted as a tension between pride (the passion for preeminence and honour) and fear (the apprehension of dishonour) which reason discerns how to resolve. But there are difficulties.

First, the resolution suggested is one-sided: fear is allayed but at the cost of Felicity. And this is a situation to be desired only by a creature who fears to be dishonoured more than he desires to be honoured, a creature content to survive in a world from which both honour and dishonour have been removed—and this is not exactly the creature Hobbes had been describing to us. In the end, it appears, all that reason can teach us is the manner in which we may escape fear, but a man compact of pride will not be disposed to accept this low-grade (if gilt-edged) security as the answer to his needs, even if he believes that to refuse it entails almost inevitable dishonour. In short, either this is a solution appropriate to the character of a more commonplace creature, one who merely desires "success in obtaining those things which a man from time to time desireth,"[25] who wants to prosper in a modest sort of way and with as little hindrance and as much help as may be from his fellows, and for whom survival in this condi-

23. See p. 133, Appendix.
24. *L.*, pp. 131–32.
25. *L.*, p. 48.

tion is more important than Joy; or Hobbes was guilty of defining human Felicity in such a manner that it is inherently impossible to be experienced by human beings as he understands them, guilty of the solecism of making the conditions of Felicity a bar to its attainment.

And secondly, we may, perhaps, enquire why, on Hobbes's reading of the situation, pride and fear should not be allowed to remain without any attempt to resolve the tension between them. No doubt, when reason speaks it may legitimately claim to be heard; for reason, no less than passion, belongs to "nature." But if (as Hobbes understood it) the office of reason is that of a servant, revealing the probable causes of events, the probable consequences of actions and the probable means by which desired ends may be attained, whence comes its authority to determine a man's choice of conduct? And if no such authority may be attributed to it, are we constrained to do more than to take note of its deliverances and then choose (with our eyes open) what we shall do? A prudent man, one set upon survival, will not easily be argued out of his prudence, and he may like to support himself with the opinion that he is acting "rationally"; but he may suddenly find his prudence deprived of its value when he sees in another (who has chosen the risky enterprise of glory) the "Joy" he has himself foregone. He will be reminded that there is such a thing as folly; and his gilt-edged security may seem a shade less attractive, a shade less adequate to human character.[26] Perhaps, even, he may dimly discern that

> There is no pleasure in the world so sweet
> As, being wise, to fall at folly's feet.

At all events (though, as we shall see, Hobbes is unjustly accused of ignoring these considerations), we may, perhaps, sus-

---

26. But against this may be set the fact that in the *civitas* there is still some opportunity for competition and taking risks; all that we are deprived of is the "joy" of success in utterly unprotected imprudence.

pect that in seeming here to recommend the pursuit of peace and the rejection of glory as "rational" conduct, he was, as on some other occasions, being forgetful of his view that "reason serves only to convince the truth (not of fact, but) of consequence"[27] and was taking improper advantage of that older meaning of "reason" in which it was recognized to have the qualities of a master or at least of an authoritative guide.

3

As it first appears, the condition of peace is merely a conclusion of natural reason. Awakened from the make-believe of vainglory and inspired by the fear of shameful death, "reason" not only reveals to men the connection between survival and peace, but also "suggesteth" the means by which this condition may be achieved and discerns its structure, which Hobbes called "the convenient articles of peace."[28] With the first (the means of achievement) we are not now concerned, but a consideration of the second discloses what Hobbes meant by "peace." There are, in all, nineteen of these articles and together they outline a condition in which the struggle for precedence is superseded, not by cooperative enterprise, but by mutual forebearance. This array of articles, said Hobbes, may, however, be "contracted into an easy sum, intelligible even to the meanest capacity, that is, *Do not to another, which thou wouldest not have done to oneself*."[29] The negative form of the maxim reveals the idiom of the moral life which Hobbes was exploring, but he interprets it (as Confucius did before him) as an injunction to have consideration for others and to avoid partiality for oneself.[30]

But a transformation has taken place. The conditions of peace,

27. *L.*, p. 292, etc.
28. *L.*, p. 98.
29. *L.*, p. 121; *E.W.*, IV, 107.
30. *Analects*, XV, 23.

first offered to us *rational theorems* concerning the nature of shameful-death-avoiding conduct (that is, as a piece of prudential wisdom), now appear as *moral obligation*. Clearly (on Hobbes's assumptions) it would be foolish, in the circumstances, not to declare for peace and not to establish it in the only manner in which it can be established; but, somehow, it has also become a dereliction of duty not to do so. Nor is this change of idiom inadvertent. For Hobbes leaves us in no doubt that he properly understood the nature of moral conduct and the difference between it and merely prudent or necessary conduct.

It is to be observed, however, that in Hobbes's vocabulary the words "good" and "evil" had (as a rule) no moral connotation. "Good" merely stood for what is desirable, that is, for whatever may be the object of human appetite; "evil" signified whatever is the object of aversion. They are, therefore, redundant words which merely repeat what is already signified in words such as "pleasurable" and "painful." When Hobbes said: "Reason declares peace to be good," he did not mean that all men *ought* to promote peace, but only that all sensible men will do so.[31] And when he said: "Every man desires his own good and his own good is peace," he could not conclude that every man *ought* to endeavour peace,[32] but only that a man who does not do so is "contradicting himself."[33] There is, it is true, something that Hobbes calls a "precept of reason," and even a "rule of reason" or a "law of reason" or a "dictate of reason," thus making it appear that what is rational is, on that account, somehow obligatory. But all the examples he gives make it clear that a "precept of reason" is only a hypothetical precept and not the equivalent of a duty. Temperance, he says, "is a precept of reason, because intemperance tends to sickness and death";[34] but temperance

31. *E.W.*, II, 48; V, 192.

32. In Hobbes's idiom it is meaningless to say that a man ought to *desire* anything, though there are occasions when he falls into this way of speaking. Cf. *L.*, p. 121.

33. Cf. *L.*, pp. 101, 548; *E.W.*, II, 12, 31.

34. *E.W.*, II, 49.

cannot be a duty unless to remain alive and well is a duty, and Hobbes is clear that these are "rights" and therefore not duties. And when he writes of the laws of Nature in general as "dictates of Reason" he makes clear that he means "sayings" or "pronouncements" of reason, and *not* "commands."[35]

But the word "justice" has a moral connotation, and it was the word Hobbes most often used when he was writing in the normative idiom: to behave morally is to do just actions, and to be a virtuous man is to have a just disposition. Nevertheless, although to behave justly is to be identified with the performance of certain actions and with refraining from others, the identification calls for some subtlety. A man's duty is to have "an unfeigned and constant endeavour"[36] to behave justly; what counts, in the first place, is the endeavour and not the external achievement. Indeed, a man may do what, on the surface, is a just action, but because it is done by chance or in pursuance of an unjust endeavour he must be considered, not to be doing justice, but merely not to be guilty; and, conversely, a man may do an injurious action, but if his endeavour is for justice, he may be technically guilty but he has not acted unjustly.[37] But it must be understood, first, that for Hobbes "endeavour" is not the same as "intention": to "endeavour" is to perform actions, to make identifiable movements, and it is, therefore, possible for others to judge of a man's "endeavour" where it might be difficult to be confident about his intention. And secondly, while it seems to me doubtful whether Hobbes held there to be an obligation to be a just man, duty is fulfilled only where a man both acts justly (that is, makes movements which constitute "endeavouring justice") and acts guiltlessly (that is, avoids doing injury).

Now, as Hobbes understood it, the object of moral endeavour is peace; what we already know to be a rational endeavour is now declared to be the object of just endeavour. Or, to amplify this

---

35. *L.,* pp. 122 *sq.*
36. *L.,* p. 121.
37. *E.W.,* II, 32; IV, 109.

definition a little, just conduct is the unfeigned and constant endeavour to acknowledge all other men as one's equal, and when considering their actions in relation to oneself to discount one's own passion and self-love.[38] The word "unfeigned" was, I think, intended to indicate that this endeavour is not moral endeavour unless it is pursued for its own sake and not, for example, in order to avoid punishment or to win an advantage for oneself. And the word "endeavour" meant not only always to intend peace, but always to act in such a manner that peace is the probable consequence of our action.

The precept we have before us is, then, that "every man *ought* to endeavour peace," and our question is, What reason or justification did Hobbes provide for this delineation of moral conduct? Why ought a man unfeignedly endeavour to keep his word, to accommodate himself to others, not to take more than his share, not to set himself up as a judge in his own cause, not display hatred and contempt towards others, to treat others as his equals and to do everything else that pertains to peace?[39] How did Hobbes bridge the gap between men's natural inclinations and what ought to be done about them? And with this question we reach the obscure heart of Hobbes's moral theory. For, not only is an answer to it the chief thing we should look for in the writings of any moralist, who normally takes his precepts from current moral opinion and himself contributes only the reasons for believing them to be true; but also, in the case of Hobbes, it is the question which his commentators have had most trouble in discovering the answer to, though some of them have pressed their conclusions upon us and dismissed those of others with remarkable confidence. Hobbes was usually so much more concerned with elucidating adequate motives or "causes" for what is alleged to be just conduct than with finding adequate

38. *L.*, pp. 118, 121.
39. *L.*, ch. xv.

reasons for calling it just, that those who seek an answer to our question are forced to use all their ingenuity.

4

There are three current readings of Hobbes's answer to this question which deserve consideration because, though none is (I believe) entirely satisfactory, each has been argued acutely and carefully and none is without plausibility.[40]

1. The first account runs something like this:[41]
Every man must either endeavour "the preservation of his own nature," or endeavour something more than this, for example, to be first in the race. To endeavour nothing at all is impossible: "to have no desire is to be dead." Now every man, in all circumstances, has the right to endeavour "the preservation of his own nature";[42] in doing so he is acting justly. And in no circumstances has any man the right to endeavour more than this (for example by indulging in useless cruelty or by desiring to be first); if he seeks what is superfluous to "the preservation of his own nature,"[43] his endeavour is unreasonable, reprehensible, and unjust because it is an endeavour for his own destruction. But to endeavour to preserve his own nature, we have seen, is precisely to endeavour peace; and to endeavour more than this to endeavour war and self-destruction. Therefore a man is just when he endeavours peace, and unjust when he endeavours war. Every man has an obligation to be just, and (in principle) he has no other obligation but to endeavour peace. In short, duty is identified with dispositions and actions which are "rational" in

40. In all, of course, there are many more than three.
41. L. Strauss, *The Political Philosophy of Hobbes.*
42. *L.,* p. 99.
43. *E.W.,* II, 45 n; *L.,* pp. 116 *sq.*

the sense of not being "self-contradictory." And Hobbes, it is
said, found support for this position in the observation that the
endeavour of a man to preserve his own nature has the approval
of conscience, and the endeavour to do more than this is disap-
proved by conscience: the feeling of guiltlessness and of guilt
attach themselves respectively to each of these endeavours.
Thus, activity which springs from fear of shameful death and is
designed to mitigate that fear alone has the approval of conscience and is obligatory.

Now, there can be no doubt that this is a moral doctrine insofar as it is an attempt to elucidate a distinction between natural
appetite and permissible appetite; it does not assimilate right to
might or duty to desire. Moreover, it is a doctrine which identifies moral conduct with prudentially rational conduct: the just
man is the man who has been tamed by fear. But if Hobbes has
said no more than this, he must be considered not to have said
enough. And, in any case, he did say something more and something different.

In the first place, the answer given here to the question, why
ought all men to endeavour peace? itself provokes a question:
we want to know why every man has an obligation only to endeavour to preserve his own nature. The whole position rests
upon the belief that Hobbes thought every man had an *obligation* to act in such a manner as not to risk his own destruction,
whereas what Hobbes said is that every man has a *right* to preserve his own nature and that a right is neither a duty nor does
it give rise to a duty of any sort.[44] Secondly, an interpretation of
Hobbes which represents him as saying that dutiful conduct is
rational conduct in the sense of being "consistent" or nonself-
contradictory conduct, and that it is dutiful because it is rational
in this (or any other) sense, must be considered wide of the
mark. There are occasions when Hobbes appealed to the principle of "noncontradiction" in order to denote what is desirable

44. *L.*, p. 99.

in conduct;[45] but, it is safe to say, he distinguished clearly between merely rational conduct and obligatory conduct. On no plausible reading of Hobbes is the Law of Nature to be considered obligatory because it represents rational conduct. Thirdly, this interpretation does not recognize moral conduct as the disinterested acknowledgement of all others as one's equal which Hobbes took to be fundamental for peace; on this showing, all endeavours for peace, however interested, would be equally just. And lastly, there is in this account a confusion between the cause of conduct alleged to be just and the reason for thinking it just. For the apprehension of shameful death and the aversion from it are not reasons why we have an obligation to endeavour peace; they are the causes or motives of our doing so. And if "reason" is added (as Hobbes added it) as a mediator between fear and pride, we have still not made our escape from the realm of causes into the realm of justifications, because "reason" for Hobbes (except where he is being unmistakably equivocal) has no prescriptive force. In short, if Hobbes said no more than this he must be considered not to have had a moral theory at all.

2. There are, however, other interpretations of Hobbes's views on this matter, which run on different lines. And we may consider next what is, perhaps, the simplest of all the current accounts. It goes as follows:

According to Hobbes, all moral obligation derives from *law;* where there is no law there is no duty and no distinction between just and unjust conduct, and where there is law in the proper sense there is an obligation to obey it upon those who come under it if there is also an adequate motive for obeying it. Now, law properly speaking (we are told) is "the command of him, that by right hath command over others";[46] or (in a more ample description) "law in general, . . . is command; nor a command of any

45. E.g. *E.W.,* II, 12, 31; *L.,* pp. 101, 548.
46. *L.,* p. 123.

man to any man; but only of him whose command is addressed to one formerly obliged to obey him."[47] And a law-maker in the proper sense is one who has acquired this antecedent authority to be obeyed by being given it, or by being acknowledged to have it, by those who are to be subject to his commands, "there being no obligation on any man, which ariseth not from some act of his own."[48] This act of authorization or acknowledgement is a necessary condition of genuine law-making authority. In other words, there can be no such thing, for Hobbes, as a "natural," unacquired, authority to make law.[49] To this, two other conditions of obligation are added: law in the proper sense can issue from a "law-maker" only when those who are obliged by it know him as the author of the law, and when they know precisely what he commands. But these conditions are, in fact, entailed in the first condition; for, no subject could know himself to be a subject without this act of authorization or acknowledgement, and it would be impossible to perform such an act and at the same time be ignorant of who the law-maker is and what he commands.

In short, it is unmistakably Hobbes's view that law is something made and that it is binding solely on account of having been made in a certain manner by a law-maker having certain characteristics; and that obligation springs only from law. Or, in other words, no command is inherently (that is, merely on account of what it commands or on account of the reasonableness of what it commands) or self-evidently binding; its obligatoriness is something to be proved or rebutted, and Hobbes told us what evidence is relevant for this proof or rebuttal. This evidence is

47. *L.*, pp. 203, 406; *E.W.*, II, 49.
48. *L.*, pp. 166, 220, 317, 403, 448; *E.W.*, II, 113, 191; IV, 148.
49. Those passages in which Hobbes seems inclined to recognize mere Omnipotence as authority to make law are not to be excluded from this condition. Omnipotence, no less than any other authoritative characteristic, is something accorded; he only is Omnipotent who is admitted or acknowledged to be so or who has been expressly accorded unlimited power. And this is true of God (except where the name God denotes merely a First Cause) no less than of men, for "God" is a name to which men have agreed to accord a certain significance. *L.*, pp. 282, 525.

solely concerned with whether or not the command is law in the proper sense, that is, whether or not it has been made by one who has authority to make it.

Now the proposition that the law of the *civitas* is law in the proper sense was, for Hobbes, not an empirical but an analytic proposition;[50] *civitas* is defined as an artificial condition of human life in which there are laws which are known to have been made by a law-maker who has acquired the authority to make them by being given it by those who are subject to him,[51] and in which what is commanded is known, and in which there is an authentic interpretation of what is commanded. And further, those who are subject to these laws have an adequate motive for their subjection. All the conditions for law in the proper sense are satisfied by civil law. Consequently (it is argued by those who defend this reading of Hobbes's writings) Hobbes's settled view was that civil laws are unquestionably obligatory, and their obligatoriness springs not from their being a reflection of some other "natural" law which carries with it "natural" duties, but solely from the character of their maker and the manner in which they have been made, promulgated, and interpreted. The question, Why am I morally bound to obey the commands of the sovereign of my *civitas*? (which, for Hobbes, is the important question) requires no other answer than, Because I, in agreement with others in a similar plight to myself, and with a common disposition to make covenants, having "authorized" him, know him indubitably to be a law-giver and know his commands as laws properly speaking.[52] Furthermore (it is argued), not only are the laws of a *civitas* laws in the proper sense, but, in a *civitas*, they are, for Hobbes, the only laws which have this character. Neither the so-called "laws" of a church, nor the so-called Laws of Na-

50. Cf. *L.*, p. 443.

51. This is true both in respect of sovereigns whose authority is by Acquisition and those who acquire it by Institution (*L.*, pp. 549 *sq.*). And it is taken by Hobbes to have been true also of the ancient "Kingdom" of the Jews (*L.*, ch. xxxv).

52. *L.*, pp. 131, 135, 166, 220, 317.

ture, are, in a *civitas*, laws in the proper sense unless and until
they have been made so by being promulgated as civil laws.[53]
Indeed, it is Hobbes's view that there is no law that is law properly speaking which is not a "civil" law in the sense of being the
command of a civil sovereign: God's laws are laws in the proper
sense only where God is a civil sovereign exercising his sovereignty through agents. The civil sovereign does not, of course,
"make" the Laws of Nature as rational theorems about human
preservation, but he does, in the strictest sense, "make" them
laws in the proper sense.[54] It may, for example, be accounted
reasonable to render unto God (where God is *not* a civil sovereign) the things that are God's and unto Caesar the things that
are Caesar's, but, according to Hobbes, this does not become a
duty until these respective spheres are defined, and, in both
cases, the definition is a matter of civil law. No doubt in a *civitas*
a subject may retain the relics of a Natural Right, but a natural
right, according to Hobbes, is not an obligation and has nothing
whatever to do with a man's duties.

On this reading of Hobbes's thoughts on moral obligation,
there remains the question whether or not he thought that men
who are not subjects of a properly constituted civil sovereign and
who therefore have no duties under a civil law nevertheless have
duties as well as rights. And this question resolves itself into the
question, where there is no civil law, is there a law which is law
in the proper sense? This is an interesting question, but for two
reasons it is not a highly important question for those who read
Hobbes in the manner we are now considering. First, Hobbes is
understood to be writing, not for savages, but for men who belong to a *civitas;* his project is to show what *their* obligations are
and whence they arise, and if he has given a reason for believing
that civil law is binding and is the only law that is binding, he
does not need to do more than this. And secondly (on the inter-

53. *L.*, pp. 205, 222, 405, 406, 469.
54. *L.*, p. 437.

pretation we are now considering) there can be no question of the obligations of civil law being derived from or being in any way connected with, another law, even if that other "law" were found, in circumstances other than those of the *civitas*, to be law in the proper sense and to impose duties upon all mankind: in a *civitas* the *only* law in the proper sense is civil law. The core of this interpretation is the belief that, for Hobbes, the *civitas* constituted not a useful addition to human life, but a transformation of the natural conditions of human life. However, the consideration of Hobbes's thoughts on obligations imposed by a law other than civil law is more appropriate in connection with another interpretation of his moral theory for which this question is central.

In the interpretation we are now considering, then, what *causes* human beings to enter into the agreement by which the civil sovereign is constituted and authorized is their fear of destruction which has been converted into a rational endeavour for peace; but they have no obligation to do so. Their *duty* to endeavour peace begins with the appearance of civil law, a law properly so-called and the only one of its kind, commanding this endeavour.

This interpretation (like any other) depends upon a certain reading of important passages in Hobbes's writings, and without calling attention to all the relevant passages it may be noticed, first, that it relies upon what must be recognized as the only intelligible reading of the passage in *Leviathan* where Hobbes maintains what may be called the sovereignty of civil law;[55] and secondly, it entails understanding the expression "whose command is addressed to one formerly obliged to obey him"[56] (used by Hobbes to define the law-giver in the proper sense) to signify "one who has already covenanted to set him up, or who has otherwise recognized him, or acknowledge him as a sovereign law-

55. *L.*, p. 205.
56. *L.*, p. 203.

maker." This, I believe, in spite of the weakening of the word "obliged" that it involves, is the most plausible reading of this expression.[57] But this reading is not without difficulties and we shall have to consider another reading of it the acceptance of which would go far to make this interpretation of Hobbes's moral theory untenable.

To this interpretation there are three main objections. First (it is observed), if the only obligation of the subject in a *civitas* is to perform the duties imposed by the law-maker whom he has (by covenant or acknowledgement) authorized, and if it is based solely upon the fact that they are genuine duties because the civil law is undoubtedly law in the proper sense and applies to the subject in a *civitas*, what, if anything, binds him to go on observing the acknowledgement or covenant which authorizes the law-maker to make law? Has he a duty to continue this acknowledgement, insofar as it can be separated from the duty to obey the laws? If not, does not Hobbes's account of moral obligation hang suspended for want of an answer to a pertinent question? And if he has such a duty, must not there be a law in the proper sense, other than civil law, which imposes it? This must be recognized as a formidable objection, but in the view of those whose views we are now considering, it is not unanswerable; indeed, there are two possible answers. First, it may be contended that there is little in Hobbes (except what is obscure or equivocal, e.g. *L.*, p. 110) to suggest that he held the making of the Covenant (besides being a prudent act) was also a moral obligation, and that "keeping the covenant" and "obeying the law" were not inseparable activities; and if there is a duty to obey the law (which there is), then there is a constructive duty to keep and protect the covenant.[58] But, secondly, if it is conceded that for there to be a duty to "keep the covenant" there must be a law imposing this duty and it cannot be the civil law itself, then, since on this interpretation there is no such "other" law in the

57. Cf. Pollock, *An Introduction to the History of the Science of Politics*, p. 65.
58. Cf. *E.W.*, II, 31; *L.*, pp. 101, 548.

proper sense (i.e. no law which is *not* based on the acknowledgement of the ruler by the subject) to be found in Hobbes's writings, we must conclude that for Hobbes there was no specific duty to keep the covenant. And why should there be? Neither Hobbes's moral theory nor any other is to be reckoned defective because it does not show every desirable action to be also a duty. For Hobbes duty is always (directly or indirectly) the activity of endeavouring peace, and to endeavour peace *is* a duty only when there is a law commanding it. To make and keep the covenant (or the acknowledgement) in which the *civitas* is set up are activities of endeavouring peace. But if, in this respect, they are eligible to become duties, it is not necessary for them to be duties; and, if they are not duties (for lack of a law commanding them) they are not, on that account, unintelligible. They are for Hobbes (on this reading) acts of prudence which are reasonable and desirable to be performed on condition that others perform them, or acts of "nobility" which make no conditions. It is, of course, true that, for Hobbes, it could never be a duty to act against one's own interest (that is, to endeavour the war of all against all), but it does not follow from this that endeavouring peace must always be a duty. In short, if Hobbes is understood to have said that there is a duty to obey the law of the *civitas* because, for the subjects of a *civitas*, it is law in the proper sense, but that there is no separate duty to make and keep the covenant or acknowledgement which sets up the civil sovereign, he is not being understood to have said anything inherently absurd: he is merely being recognized to have said that there is a proper use for the word "duty," but that what holds the *civitas* together is not "duty" (except, for example, the duty imposed by a law against treason) but either self-interest instructed by reason, or the nobility which is too proud to calculate the possible loss entailed in obedience to a "sovereign" who lacks power to enforce his commands.[59]

59. In the Conclusion of *Leviathan* (p. 548) Hobbes added a twentieth Law of Nature, namely, "that every man is bound by Nature, as much as in him lieth, to protect in Warre, the Authority, by which he himself is protected in time of Peace." And

The second objection is as follows: it is alleged that, for Hobbes, rational behaviour is endeavouring peace, and that this becomes a duty if and when it is commanded by law in the proper sense. Further, since civil law *is* law in the proper sense and the only law in the proper sense (owing its propriety not to its being a reflection of some other, superior, and equally proper law, but solely to the manner in which it has been made, published, and authentically interpreted) and commands its subjects to endeavour peace, these have a duty (which persons in other circumstances have not) of "endeavouring peace." But (it is objected) this is not an accurate account of the situation. What, even for Hobbes, the civil law commands is not merely that a man shall "endeavour peace" but that he shall perform specific actions and refrain from others: it is no defence for the lawbreaker to say, "I am endeavouring peace," if he neglects to do what the law commands or does what it forbids. The answer to this objection is, however, that, for Hobbes, "endeavouring peace" was always performing specific acts (and not merely having peaceful intentions or a generally peaceful disposition); to be disposed in a certain direction is to make movements in that direction. And, while reason acquaints all but madmen and children with the general pattern of acts which may be expected to promote a peaceful condition of human life, it is the province of law to decide what acts, in specific circumstances, are necessary to a condition of peace and to impose them as duties.[60] When "endeavouring peace" is a *duty*, it is always the duty of obeying a law, and a law is always a set of specific commands and prohibitions. Hence, the duty of endeavouring peace is indistinguishable from the duty of performing the acts prescribed by law: a man cannot at the same time "endeavour peace" and do what

---

he explains that this is so because not to act in this way would be self-contradictory. But to demonstrate self-consistency is not to demonstrate duty: and the conduct which is here asserted to be self-consistent becomes a duty only when there is a law in the proper sense imposing it, and for members of a *civitas* such a law must be a civil law.

60. *L.*, p. 136.

the law forbids, though he may do so by actions which the law does not require of him—by being benevolent, for example. But his *duty* to "endeavour peace" is a duty to obey the law, that is, to be both just and guiltless.

The third objection is that Hobbes is often to be found writing about "natural laws" and writing about them as if he considered them to be laws in the proper sense and capable of imposing a "natural obligation" upon all men to endeavour peace, and any account of Hobbes's moral theory which ignores this is implausible. This, again, is not easily to be disposed of. It is true that Hobbes repeatedly and clearly asserted that Natural Laws are not properly speaking laws at all except where they appear as the commands of a law-giver *who owes his authority to a covenant or an acknowledgement;* apart from this, they are only "qualities which dispose men to peace and order," "dictates," "conclusions," or "theorems" of natural reason "suggesting" the conduct which belongs to a condition of peace and therefore the rational (but not the moral) foundation of the *civitas*.[61] But these assertions are partnered by others capable of being interpreted to mean that the Laws of Nature themselves impose obligations upon all men (rulers included), and even that the obligation of the subject to obey the laws of his *civitas* derives from the duty he has under one or more of these natural laws.[62] However, since the view that Hobbes believed Natural Law to be law in the proper sense and to be the source of all moral obligation is the central theme of the third important account of Hobbes's moral theory, the force of this objection to this account will best be considered in that connection.

3. This third interpretation begins at the same place as the one we have just considered.[63] It recognizes that, for Hobbes, all moral obligation derives from a law of some sort: where there is

61. *L.,* pp. 97, 122, 205, 211, etc.; *E.W.,* II, 49–50, etc.
62. *L.,* pp. 99, 110, 121, 203, 258–59, 273, 363.; *E.W.,* II, 46, 47, 190, 200.
63. H. Warrender, *The Political Philosophy of Hobbes;* J. M. Brown, *Political Studies,* Vol. I, No. 1; Vol. II, No. 2.

authentic law there is, on that account, duty; where there is no law there is no duty. Consequently, endeavouring peace can be shown to be a duty upon all men if there is a valid and universally applicable law commanding it. So far, I think there can be no serious disagreement about what Hobbes thought. But it is now contended that the Law of Nature itself and without further qualification is, in Hobbes's view, a valid, universal, and perpetually operative law imposing this duty upon all men. Every interpreter of Hobbes recognizes that what Hobbes called the Laws of Nature and what he called "the convenient articles of peace" are, in respect of content, the same thing and that they are the "suggestions" or conclusions of reason about the preservation of human life. What is asserted now is that Hobbes also believed them to be laws in the proper sense; namely, that their author is known and that he has acquired an antecedent right to command, that they have been published and are known, that there is an authentic interpretation of them, and that those who have a duty to obey have a sufficient motive for doing so. And the conclusion suggested is that endeavouring peace was, for Hobbes, an obligation laid upon all men by a Law of Nature and that any further obligation there may be to obey the laws of the *civitas*, or to obey covenanted commands, derives from this natural and universal obligation.[64]

Now, it is not to be denied that there are expressions and passages in Hobbes's writings which appear to be designed to make us believe that this is his view, but before we accept them at their face value we must consider in detail whether Hobbes also held

---

64. There are further subtleties in some versions of this interpretation which I do not propose to consider here because, whether or not they can be shown to be components of Hobbes's view of things, they do not affect the main point. For example, the suggestion that the *civitas* is a condition in which the obligation to endeavour peace (already imposed by a Natural Law) is "validated." Clearly, this suggestion is cogent only when it is believed that, for Hobbes, the Law of Nature is law in the proper sense. Our main concern is with the question: Is the Law of Nature, by itself and without qualification of circumstances or persons, law in the proper sense and capable of imposing upon all mankind the duty of "endeavouring peace"?

the beliefs which are for him certainly entailed in this view. And if we find this not to be the case, it may be thought that these passages are eligible for some other interpretation, or that we must be content to have detected what, on any reading, is a notable incoherence in his writings.

The direction of our first enquiry is unmistakable. Since, according to Hobbes, the obligation a law imposes is due not to the law itself but to its author,[65] who must not only be known as its author but known also to have a right to command, our first enquiry must be: Did Hobbes believe the Law of Nature to have an author known as such to all mankind? And if so, who did he think was its author and in what manner did he think this author was known to be the maker of this law? And, together with this, we may appropriately consider what thoughts Hobbes's writings disclose about the right of this author to make this law. The answer urged upon us in the interpretation we are now considering is that Hobbes unmistakably believed the Law of Nature to have an author who is naturally known to all men as such; that this author is God himself; and that his right to legislate derives, not from his having created those who should obey his commands, but from his Omnipotence.[66] The Law of Nature, it is contended, is law in the proper sense; it is binding upon all men in all circumstances because it is known to be the command of an Omnipotent God.

The first difficulty which stands in the way of our accepting this interpretation is that it must remain exceedingly doubtful (to say the least) whether Hobbes thought that our natural knowledge includes (or could possibly include) a knowledge of God as the author of imperative laws for human conduct. He

65. E.g. *E.W.*, II, 191 *sq.*

66. This excludes two otherwise possible views. First, that it is a duty to conform to the Law of Nature because it is self-evidently rational or because it is axiomatically obligatory: there is, I think, no plausible reading of Hobbes in which the Law of Nature is recognized to be obligatory except in respect of its authorship. And secondly, that the Law of Nature is obligatory on account of its authorship, but that the author is not God. For this third interpretation of Hobbes's theory, God is essential.

reasoned thus about the word "God": divinities appear first as projections of human fear consequent upon our frequent ignorance of the causes of the good and ill fortunes which befall us, but the notion of "one God, Infinite and Omnipotent" derives, not from our fears, but from our curiosity about "the causes of natural bodies, their several virtues and operations": in tracing these causes backwards we unavoidably "come to this, that there must be one First Mover; that is, a First, and Eternal cause of all things; which is that which men mean by the name of God."[67] It is this God, then, a necessary hypothesis, of whom we may be said, in the first place, to have natural knowledge. And in virtue of the Omnipotence of this God (his "rule" as a First Cause being inescapable and absolute) we may speak of him as "King of all the earth," and we may speak of the earth as his natural Kingdom and everything on earth as his natural subject; but if we do speak in this manner, we must recognize that we are using the words "King" and "Kingdom" in only a metaphorical sense.[68]

Nevertheless, the name God may also be used with another signification in which he may be said to be a "King" and to have a natural Kingdom and natural subjects in the proper meaning of these expressions: he is a genuine ruler over those "that believe that there is a God that governeth the world, and hath given Praecepts, and propounded Rewards and Punishments to Mankind."[69] But, about this there are two observations to be made. First, these beliefs fall short of natural knowledge, which is confined (in this connection) to the necessary hypothesis of God as the Omnipotent First Cause;[70] the "providential" God is no less a "projection" of human thought than the God who is the First Cause, but whereas the First Cause is a projection of human

---

67. *L.*, p. 83.

68. *L.*, pp. 90, 314 *sq.*

69. *L.*, pp. 274, 314. This is a necessary condition, but (as we shall see shortly) the necessary and sufficient condition is that they should not only "believe" in a God of this sort, but that they should have acknowledged him as *their* ruler.

70. According to Hobbes we have no natural knowledge of God's nature, or of a life after death. *L.*, p. 113.

reason, the providential God is a projection of human desire.[71] And secondly, since these beliefs about a "providential" God are avowedly *not* common to all mankind,[72] God's natural subjects (i.e. those who have an obligation to obey his commands) are those only who have acknowledged a "providential" God concerned with human conduct and who hope for his rewards and fear his punishments. (And it may be remarked here, in passing, that this circumstance qualifies the distinction Hobbes was apt to make between God's natural subjects and his subjects by covenant: the only proper understanding of the expression "Kingdom of God" is when it is taken to signify "a Commonwealth, instituted (by the consent of those who were to be subject thereto) for their Civil Government"[73]). The law which the subjects of this God are bound to obey is the Law of Nature,[74] they have a duty always to endeavour peace. Others, it is true, may feel the weight of this law, may find themselves in receipt of pleasure for following its precepts or pain for not doing so, but these have no moral obligation to obey it and this pleasure is not a reward and this pain is not a punishment.

It would appear, then, that, according to Hobbes, God as the author of a law imposing the duty of endeavouring peace, is the ruler, not of all mankind, but only of those who acknowledge him in this character and therefore know him as its author; and this acknowledgement is a matter of "belief," not of natural knowledge.[75] It is a loose way of talking to say that Hobbes anywhere

71. *L.*, p. 525.
72. *L.*, p. 275. This is not because some men are atheists. An "atheist," according to Hobbes, is an ill-reasoner who fails to arrive at the hypothesis of a First Cause and is only inferentially a man who does not believe in a "providential" God concerned with human conduct. Hobbes recognizes various classes of person in this respect—Atheists; those who recognize a First Cause but do not believe in a "providential" God; the insane and the immature; and those who recognize a First Cause and believe in a "providential" God. It is only those who compose the last of these classes who are obliged by the Law of Nature.
73. *L.*, p. 317, etc. But *E.W.*, II, 206, should be noticed.
74. *L.*, p. 276.
75. Cf. *L.*, p. 300.

said that we are obliged by the Laws of Nature because they are the Laws of God; what he said is that we would be obliged by them if they were laws in the proper sense, and that they are laws in the proper sense only if they are known to have been made by God.[76] And this means that they are laws in the proper sense only to those who know them to have been made by God. And who are these persons? Certainly not all mankind; and certainly only those of mankind who have acknowledged God to be maker of this law. The proposition, then, that Hobbes thought the Law of Nature to be law in the proper sense and to bind all mankind to an endeavour for peace, cannot seriously be entertained, whatever detached expressions (most of them ambiguous) there may be in his writings to support it.[77]

But further, if it is clear that even God's so-called "natural subjects" can have no natural knowledge of God as the author of a universally binding precept to endeavour peace, it is clear also that Hobbes did not allow them to have any other sort of knowledge of God as the author of a Law of Nature of this kind. He expressly affirmed that if they claim to know God as the author of a law imposing the duty of endeavouring peace on all mankind by means of "Sense Supernatural" (or "Revelation," or "Inspiration") their claim must be disallowed;[78] whatever else "Sense Supernatural" might acquaint a man with, it cannot acquaint him with a universal law or with God as the author of a universal law. Nor can "Prophecy" supply what "natural knowledge" and "Sense Supernatural" have failed to supply. It is true that by "Faith" a man may know God as the author of a law, but what "Faith" can show us is not God as the author of a "Natural Law" imposing duties on all men, but God as the author of a "Positive Law" enjoining duties only upon those who by indirect covenant have acknowledged him as their ruler and have authorized him by their consent. In short, only where the endeavour for peace

76. *L.,* p. 403.
77. E.g. *L.,* pp. 315, 363.
78. *L.,* p. 275.

is enjoined by a positive law does it become a duty, this law alone being law in the proper sense as having a known author; and this law is binding only upon those who know its author.

The question, Did Hobbes think the Law of Nature to be law in the proper sense in respect of having a known author? resolves itself into the question, Who among mankind, because they know God as the author of a precept to endeavour peace, did Hobbes think to be bound to obey this precept? And in answering this question, we have found that Hobbes's much advertised distinction between God's "natural subjects" and his subjects by covenant or acknowledgement is not as firmly based as we at first supposed: God's only "Kingdom," in the proper sense, is a *civitas* in which God is owned as the author of the *civil* law. And the same conclusion appears when we consider the related question, By what authority does God impose this obligation? In the interpretation of Hobbes's writings we are now considering the authority of God over his so-called "natural subjects" is said to derive from Irresistible Power and consequently to be an authority to make law for all mankind.[79] But this cannot be so, whatever Hobbes seems to have said in these passages and elsewhere. Omnipotence or Irresistible Power is the characteristic of God as "the First, and Eternal Cause of all things," but this God is not a law-maker or a "ruler," and we have been warned that to speak of him as a "King" and as having a "Kingdom" is to speak metaphorically. The God who appears as, in the proper sense, a "ruler" (the imposer of authentic obligations) is not the "ruler" of everybody and everything in the world, but only of "as many of mankind as acknowledge his Providence." It is in their acknowledgement of him as their ruler that he comes to be known as the author of law properly speaking; this acknowledgement is the necessary "act" from which all obligation "ariseth" because it is the act without which the ruler remains unknown.[80] Not

79. *L.*, pp. 90, 276, 315, 474, 551; *E.W.*, II, 209; VI, 170.
80. *L.*, pp. 97, 166, 317.

Omnipotence, then, but a covenant or an acknowledgement is the spring of God's authority to make laws in the proper sense.

Now, besides having a known author, the Law of Nature, if it is to be law in the proper sense, must have two other characteristics; namely, it must be known or knowable by those who are obliged to obey it (that is, it must have been in some manner "published" or "declared"), and there must be an "authentique interpretation" of it. Did Hobbes think that the Law of Nature has these characteristics?

In regard to the first, the interpretation of Hobbes we are now considering appears to be in no difficulty: it relies upon Hobbes's statements that the Law of Nature is declared by God to his natural subjects in the "Dictates of Natural Reason" or of "Right Reason"; that it is known in this manner "without other word of God"; and that a sufficient knowledge of it is available even to those whose power of reasoning is not very conspicuous.[81] But, it may be asked, how can a man know "by the Dictates of Right Reason" that the endeavour for peace is a command emanating from a proper authority, and therefore imposing upon him a duty to obey, when "Reason" (being, according to Hobbes, the power of discerning the probable causes of given occurrences or the probable effects of given actions or movements serving "to convince the truth (not of fact, but) of consequence")[82] can neither itself supply, nor be the means of ascertaining, categorical injunctions? How can God "declare his laws" (as *laws* and not merely as theorems) to mankind in "the Dictates of Natural Reason"? And the answer to these enquiries is clear: nobody holding Hobbes's views about the nature of "reason" could possibly hold God to be able to do anything of the sort. And if God cannot do this, then the whole idea of the Law of Nature being law in the proper sense and imposing duties on all mankind because it is known and known to be the law of God, collapses. No doubt

81. *L.*, pp. 225, 275, 277, 554.
82. *L.*, p. 292; *E.W.*, I, 3.

there are occasions when Hobbes encourages us to think that he
thought the Law of Nature was naturally known, *as a law in the
proper sense* imposing upon all mankind the duty of endeavouring peace; he was not above speaking of "natural duties"[83]
(though he refused to recognize the expression "natural justice"),[84] and we shall have to consider later why he encourages
us to think in this manner. But there is also no doubt that, according to his own understanding of "Reason," all that he may
legitimately think is that the Law of Nature *as a set of theorems
about human preservation* is known to all mankind in this manner.[85] In default, then, of evidence from the writings of Hobbes
other than these unmistakably equivocal references to "natural
reason," we must conclude that the Law of Nature is not law in
the proper sense, and that the duty to endeavour peace is not
naturally known either to all mankind or even to God's so-called
"natural subjects." What *is* known is the duty to endeavour peace
when it is recognized as imposed by the positive law of God upon
those who by indirect covenant have acknowledged his authority
to impose this duty; it is known to them because it has been
published to them either in the "propheticall" word of God, or
in the positive law of the *civitas;* and in the *civitas* "prophecy"
and the command of the Sovereign are not to be distinguished,
for the Civil Sovereign is "God's prophet."[86]

83. *L.,* p. 277.
84. *E.W.,* II, vi.
85. *L.,* p. 286. The expression "Right Reason" belongs to a well-established view
of things in which it was supposed that "reason," a "divine spark," could acquaint
mankind with at least some of its moral duties, but it is a view of things which Hobbes
on most occasions is concerned expressly to deny. For Hobbes "our natural reason"
is "the undoubted word of God" (*L.,* p. 286), but what it conveys is hypothetical
information about causes and effects, not categorical information about duties; and
there is even some inconsistency in his use of the expression "*our* reason"—"reason,"
properly speaking, is, for him, the power of reasoning, i.e. of drawing warrantable
conclusions. The appearance, then, of this expression "Right Reason" in Hobbes's
writings is a signal to the attentive reader to be on his guard and to suspect equivocation.
86. *L.,* p. 337.

The third characteristic of law in the proper sense is the existence of an "authentique interpretation" of its meaning;[87] and this the Law of Nature manifestly lacks unless it is supplied by some positive and acknowledged authority, such as a civil sovereign or a "prophet" instructed by God and acknowledged by his followers:[88] God himself cannot be the interpreter of the Law of Nature any more than he can be the interpreter of his Scriptural "word." In short, for Hobbes, there can be no interpreter or interpretation of the Law of Nature which is at once "natural" or "uncovenanted" and "authentique." It is true that the "natural reason" or the "conscience" of private men may be represented as interpreters of the Law of Nature,[89] but they cannot be thought to supply an "authentique" interpretation of it as a law. When each man is his own interpreter, not only is it impossible to exclude the partiality of passion (and conscience, in the end, is only a man's good opinion of what he has done or is inclined to do), but the obligation of the law thus interpreted ceases to be a universal obligation to endeavour peace and becomes, at most, an obligation upon each man to obey his own *bona fide* version of the law—which is not enough. A law which may be different for each man under "it" is not a law at all but merely a multiplicity of opinions about how the legislator (in this case, God) wishes us to behave.[90] There is, in fact, no law where there is no *common* authority to declare and interpret it.[91] Nor does it mend matters to suggest that each man is responsible to God for the *bona fide* character of his interpretation: this responsibility could only apply to that fraction of mankind who believed in a providential God concerned with human conduct.

87. *L.*, pp. 211 *sq.*, 534; *E.W.*, II, 220.
88. *L.*, pp. 85, 317.
89. *L.*, p. 249.
90. Cf. *L.*, pp. 453, 531, 534. Compare Hobbes's rejection of "writers" and "books of Moral Philosophy" as authentic interpreters of the civil law (*L.*, p. 212). An "authentique" interpretation must be single and authoritative, and without an interpretation there is no known law and therefore no law and no duty.
91. *L.*, p. 98.

The enquiry provoked by the interpretation of Hobbes's writings we are now considering has led us to the view that the question, Has the Law of Nature, according to Hobbes, the necessary and sufficient characteristics of a law in the proper sense binding all mankind to the duty of endeavouring peace? or (in another form) Is the duty of endeavouring peace a "natural," uncovenanted duty, binding upon all men? must be answered in the negative. But this enquiry has also suggested that perhaps the more relevant questions are, In what circumstances did Hobbes think the Law of Nature acquires these characteristics? and, To whom is the endeavour for peace not only a rational course of conduct for those intent upon survival but a morally binding injunction? For, although Hobbes said much that pushes our thoughts in another direction, it seems clear that for him the Law of Nature possessed these characteristics only in certain circumstances and imposed duties only upon certain persons. In general, these circumstances are those in which to endeavour peace has become a rule of positive law, human or divine; and, in general, the persons bound are those only who know the author of this law and have acknowledged his authority to make it.[92] This seems to correspond with what I take to be Hobbes's deepest conviction about moral duties; namely, that there can be "no obligation upon any man which ariseth not from some act of his own."[93] But the bearing of this principle is not that, for

---

92. Hobbes, it is well known, distinguished between two classes of obligation— *in foro interno* and *in foro externo*. This distinction has been elucidated with great care and subtlety by Mr. Warrender, but it will be agreed that it is subsidiary to the question we are now concerned with, namely: What, in Hobbes's view, are the necessary conditions of obligation of any sort? Consequently I do not propose to go into it here. It may, however, be remarked that Mr. Warrender's view that Hobbes held that, *in the State of Nature*, the Laws of Nature bind always *in foro interno*, and *in foro externo* not always (Warrender, p. 52; *L.*, p. 121), is not quite convincing. What Hobbes must be understood to be saying is that the Laws of Nature, *where they are laws in the proper sense*, oblige always *in foro interno* and *in foro externo* not always. Is it not going further than the text warrants to interpret "always" as meaning "in all conditions of human life," including the State of Nature?

93. *L.*, pp. 314, 317, 403, 448.

Hobbes, the choice of him who is obliged creates the duty, but that where there has been no choice (covenant or acknowledgement) there is no known law-giver and therefore no law in the proper sense and no duty. And it is a principle which seems to me to exclude the possibility of "natural" (that is, uncovenanted) duties. The necessary "act" may be the acknowledgement of God in the belief in a "providential" God concerned with human conduct; but, for those who live in a *civitas*, it is the act which creates and authorizes the civil sovereign because, for such persons, there are no duties which do not reach them as the commands of this sovereign.

There may be other and more obscure thoughts to be taken into account, but it seems to me certain that Hobbes thought that, whatever may or may not belong to other conditions of human circumstance, the *civitas* is unquestionably a condition in which there is a law in the proper sense[94] (namely, the civil law), in which this law is the only law in the proper sense, and in which it is the duty of all subjects to endeavour peace. The reading of Hobbes in which this covenanted duty derives from a "natural" duty, imposed antecedently upon all mankind by an independent and perpetually operative Law of Nature, ignores so many of Hobbes's conclusions about God, "reason," human knowledge, "the signification of words," and the conditions of moral obligation, that what it explains is little compared with what it leaves unaccounted for, and cannot be accepted as a satisfactory account. And besides these fundamental discrepancies, perhaps the most fertile source of the misunderstanding reflected in this interpretation is the confusion (for which Hobbes is responsible) between what he said about the "Laws of Nature" as "theorems concerning what conduceth to the conservation and defence" of mankind (namely, their availability to natural reason and their unquestionable intelligibility to even the meanest intellect) and

94. *L.,* p. 443.

what he said about them as morally binding injunctions—the confusion between reason which teaches and laws which enjoin.

5

It is safe to say that every interpretation of Hobbes's moral theory leaves something that Hobbes wrote imperfectly accounted for. But it is reasonable to distinguish between those interpretations which conflict with some (perhaps, many and repeated) detached statements in the writings, and those which conflict with what may, perhaps, be considered the structural principles of Hobbes's view of things, though it is difficult to decide where to draw the line. Of the interpretations we have before us, the first seems to me the least possible to accept, and the second (in which duty is understood to be an endeavour for peace according to the laws of the *civitas*) to be the most plausible because it conflicts least with what I take to be the structural principles of Hobbes's philosophy. Nevertheless, it must be acknowledged that Hobbes's statements about "natural" duties imposed by a Natural Law (which are the central theme of the third interpretation) are not to be regarded as mere inadvertencies. It is true that they are inconsistent with some of Hobbes's most cherished principles, but they are far too numerous to be merely ignored; indeed, Mr. Warrender has shown that, if they are abstracted from the whole, they are capable of composing together a tolerably complete moral theory. The situation we have on our hands (as I understand it) is, then, a set of philosophical writings in which there appear (not side by side, but almost inextricably mixed) a theory of moral obligation at once original and consistent with the other philosophical novelties to be found in them, and another account of moral obligation the vocabulary and general principles of which are conventional (though there are original touches of detail); and anyone disposed to find the one more significant than the other[95] may be expected to offer a more plausible explanation of the presence of what he finds less significant than that it springs merely from the confusion of Hobbes's thoughts. No doubt there is confusion at some points, but the presence of these two theories of obligation cannot be taken as an example of mere confusion.

Our question, in general, is: Why did Hobbes, in an enterprise designed to elucidate the ground and character of the obligations entailed in living in a *civitas,* run together two strikingly different (and at some points contradictory) accounts of moral obligation? And, in detail, our puzzle is to account for the discrepancies which appear in his writings of which the following are a brief selection.

1. He tells us that in nature "every man has a right to everything; even to another's body," a right to govern himself according to his own judgement, "to do anything he liketh," and to preserve himself in any manner that he finds expedient.[96] And he tells us that in nature every man has a "natural" obligation to endeavour peace, imposed by a Natural Law which is the command of an omnipotent God.

2. He tells us that "Reason" serves only to convince the truth (not of fact, but) of consequence,"[97] that it deals only in hypothetical propositions about causes and effects, that its business in human conduct is to suggest fit means for achieving desired ends, and that nothing is obligatory on account of being reasonable; but he tells us also that the Laws of Nature, as laws and not

---

95. Besides the other reasons I have already stated for finding less to object to in the first of these two than the second, as an interpretation of Hobbes's writings, some weight may perhaps be given to the fact that Hobbes believed what he had written on the subject of moral obligation would appear offensively eccentric to his contemporaries (e.g. *L.,* p. 557), and he could scarcely have believed this if his theory were of the character Mr. Warrender attributes to it.

96. *L.,* p. 99.

97. *L.,* p. 292, etc.

merely as hypothetical conclusions about human preservation, are made known to us in "the dictates of natural reason."[98]

3. He tells us that, by means of reason, we may know God as the author of a moral law; and he tells us also that by reason we can know nothing whatever about God as the author of a moral law (or about his rewards and punishments in another life), but may know God only as a First Cause.

4. He tells that "our obligation to civil obedience . . . is before all civil law,"[99] and suggests that it is a "natural" and universal obligation and derives from it an obligation not to rebel against the civil sovereign; but elsewhere he denies the universality of this "natural" obligation and specifies a class of person to whom it applies and makes it rest upon a covenant or an acknowledgement.

5. He asserts the independent *authority* of both Natural Law and Scripture, the one based on reason and the other on revelation, but elsewhere he tells us that, as members of a *civitas*, the *authority* of Natural Law derives from the imprimatur of the civil sovereign and that the precepts of Scripture are what the civil sovereign says they are.

6. He uses the word "precept" of reason as an alternative to the expression "general rule" of reason[100] to describe the first Law of Nature in an account which ends by denying that the prescriptive character of Natural Law has anything to do with its reasonableness.[101]

7. He uses the expression "natural Laws" both when he means to denote the hypothetical conclusions of human reason about human self-preservation and to denote obligations imposed by God upon those who believe in a providential God and obligations alleged to be imposed by God upon all men except

98. *L.*, p. 275, etc.
99. *E.W.*, II, 200.
100. *L.*, p. 100.
101. *L.*, p. 122.

atheists(?), lunatics, and children. This is a manner of speaking which is almost a confession of a design to confuse.

8. He says that a sovereign (without qualification) is obliged by the Law of Nature to "procure the safety (and welfare) of the people" and must "render an account thereof to God, the Author of the Law, and to none but him";[102] but, on his own showing (and apart from numerous other difficulties), that is at best true of a sovereign who belongs to that class of person who believes in a providential God concerned with human conduct, a class which (in Hobbes's writings) it is exceedingly difficult to distinguish from that of Christian believers.

9. He makes great play with a distinction between "God's natural kingdom" and his "natural subjects," and then tells us that the word "kingdom" and the word "subject" are merely metaphorical expressions in default of the "artifice" of a "covenant."

10. He distinguishes between "the first Founders, and Legislators of Commonwealths among the Gentiles"[103] who, in order to promote civil obedience and peace, encourage their subjects to believe the civil law has divine sanction, and the situation (as among the ancient Jews) where "God himself" is said to establish a kingdom by covenant; but he ignores the fact that all that he has said about God and human imagination brands the expression "God himself" as meaningless: God "is" what he is believed or "dreamed" to be, and he "does" what he is believed or "dreamed" to do.

Some commentators have believed themselves to have satisfactorily resolved some of these examples of discrepancy without having to resort to a general explanation, and perhaps the most notable of these resolutions is that attempted by Mr. Warrender in respect of *Leviathan*, p. 205.[104] But even that cannot be considered successful. He finds in this passage a *reductio ad absurdum* of natural-law theory which he conjectures Hobbes

102. *L.*, p. 258.
103. *L.*, pp. 89–90.
104. Warrender, p. 167.

could not have intended, and he rejects what must be recognized as the literal meaning of the passage because he cannot bring himself to believe that Hobbes (who certainly both asserts and denies them elsewhere) could have concurred with its entailments. But whatever success or lack of success commentators have had in resolving some of the more superficial discrepancies of Hobbes's writings, there remains a core of discrepancy impervious to this kind of treatment, and we are provoked to seek a general explanation more plausible than mere native confusion of mind, careless reasoning, and a propensity to exaggeration.

Hobbes's writings on civil obedience (and *Leviathan* in particular) may be taken to have a twofold purpose. It would appear that his project was to display a theory of obligation consistent with the tenets of his general philosophy and with his reading of human nature; and also to show his contemporaries where their civil duties lay and why they lay there, in order to combat the confusion and anarchical tendencies of current thought and conduct.[105] The first of these enterprises is an exercise in logic, and it is appropriately conducted in the vocabulary which Hobbes had made his own. The second, on the other hand, could not be successful unless it were framed in the idiom and the vocabulary of current political theory and thus present a doctrine whose novelties (if any) were assimilated to current prejudices about moral conduct. Now, as it turned out, these two enterprises (which in a more conventional writer might have been run together without notable discrepancy) conflicted with one another, not in matters of peripheral importance but in matters of central

105. If we distinguish (as we may) between an account of the dispositions and actions alleged to be morally obligatory and a doctrine designed to display the reason why whatever is believed to be obligatory is so, it may be observed, first, that, insofar as Hobbes was engaged in recommending new duties (which he is loth to do, *E.W.*, II, xxii), they were not inventions of his own but were the duties inherent in the emerging conditions of a modern State where governing is recognized as a sovereign activity; and secondly, that the two enterprises upon which Hobbes was (on this reading of him) engaged conflict (where they do conflict) not notably in respect of the duties recognized but in respect of the reason given for their being duties.

importance. Hooker, in an earlier generation, had found it possible to expound a doctrine of civil obedience, not very unlike Hobbes's more conventional theory, by making a few adjustments in the current natural-law theory, and Hobbes may be read (in one of his moods) as attempting the same sort of enterprise, though his adjustments were more radical and did not escape giving offence. But no conceivable adjustment of this conventional natural-law doctrine could result in an account of civil obligation even remotely compatible with his general philosophy. In short, if we have to choose between an explanation of the more important discrepancies in Hobbes's writing in terms of mere confusion or an explanation in terms of artful equivocation, I think the probability lies with the latter.

And if we do settle for an explanation of this sort, which recognizes Hobbes to have two doctrines, one for the initiated (those whose heads were strong enough to withstand the giddiness provoked by his scepticism) and the other for the ordinary man who must be spoken to in an idiom and a vocabulary he is accustomed to, and to whom novelties (both in respect of duties and in respect of their grounds) must be made to appear commonplaces, we are not attributing a unique and hitherto unheard of character to *Leviathan*. Numerous other writers on these topics (Plato, for example, Machiavelli, and even Bentham) were the authors of works which contain at once, and imperfectly distinguished from one another, an esoteric and an exoteric doctrine; and the view that matters of this sort (indeed, political questions generally) are "mysteries" to be discussed candidly and directly only with the initiated goes back to the beginnings of political speculation and was by no means dead in the seventeenth century.

I do not suppose that this account of Hobbes's thoughts on obligation will commend itself to everyone, and in the nature of the case it cannot be demonstrated to be true. But what appears to me probable is that the discrepancies in Hobbes's writings are of a character to require some such general explanation.

6

Our study of Hobbes has reached some conclusions which most readers will find difficult to avoid. It seems clear that he believed that a rational disposition in human beings was to be identified as an endeavour for peace. And peace meant acknowledging all others as our equal, keeping our promises, not displaying contempt and hatred, and not endeavouring to outdo all others in order to have the elation of being recognized to occupy first place. This manner of living is suggested by reason, which also suggests the means by which it may be instituted and maintained: it is the *civitas*. The reward of its accomplishment is emancipation from the constant fear of violent and shameful death at the hands of other men. And, so far, the sufficient *cause* or *motive* for endeavouring peace is found in fear of shameful death: fear prompts reason and reason discloses what must be done to avoid the circumstances which generate fear.

We have looked further to find if Hobbes had anything to say in support of his view that this endeavour is, in fact, not only reasonable, but also just—that is, morally obligatory. Here, we have observed, first, that Hobbes was certainly capable of distinguishing between the sufficient causes for human conduct and the reasons which may be given in justification of it. And further, we have observed the sort of reason which Hobbes considered adequate; namely, the existence of a law in the proper sense commanding this endeavour. Beyond this, there lies a region difficult to map. And the best an explorer can do is to determine what he thinks to be its more significant features and to give his reasons for preferring these to others. And this is what I have done. But there is still something more to be said.

The morality we have seen Hobbes to be defending is the morality of the tame man. It is still true that the greatest stimulus to the vital movement of the heart is the elation generated by being continuously recognized to be superior. But this greatest good must be foregone: pride, even when it does not degenerate into vainglory, is too dangerous a passion to be allowed, even if its suppression somewhat dims the brilliance of life.

But, in the writings of Hobbes there is another line of argument, not extensively elaborated, but enough to push our thoughts in a different direction. In this line of thought the just disposition is still recognized to be an endeavour for peace and what is sought is still emancipation from the fear of violent and shameful death at the hands of other men, but the desired condition is to be attained, not by proud man, awakened by fear, surrendering his pride and becoming (by covenant) tame man, but by the moralization of pride itself. How can this happen?

Let us suppose a man of the character Hobbes supposed all men to be: a man unavoidably his own best friend and (on account of his weakness) subject to the fear of finding himself shamed and dishonoured and even killed. But let us also suppose that the preponderant passion of this man remains pride rather than fear; that he is a man who would find greater shame in the meanness of settling for mere survival than in suffering the dishonour of being recognized a failure; a man whose disposition is to overcome fear not by reason (that is, by seeking a secure condition of external human circumstances) but by his own courage; a man not at all without imperfections and not deceived about himself, but who is proud enough to be spared the sorrow of his imperfections and the illusion of his achievements; not exactly a hero, too negligent for that, but perhaps with a touch of careless heroism about him; a man, in short, who (in Montaigne's phrase) "knows how to belong to himself," and who, if fortune turned out so, would feel no shame in the epitaph:

> Par délicatesse
> J'ai perdu ma vie.

Now, a man of this sort would not lack stimulus for the vital movement of his heart, but he is in a high degree self-moved.

His endeavour is for peace; and if the peace he enjoys is largely his own unaided achievement and is secure against the mishaps that may befall him, it is not in any way unfriendly to the peace of other men of a different kind. There is nothing hostile in his conduct, nothing in it to provoke hostility, nothing censorious. What he achieves for himself and what he contributes to a common life is a complete alternative to what others may achieve by means of agreement inspired by fear and dictated by reason; for, if the unavoidable endeavour of every man is for self-preservation, and if self-preservation is interpreted (as Hobbes interprets it), not as immunity from death but from the fear of shameful death, then this man achieves in one manner (by courage) what others may achieve in another (by rational calculation). And, unlike others, he not only abstains from doing injury but is able to be indifferent to having to suffer it from others. In short, although this character looks, at first sight, much more like the *âme forte* of Vauvenargues than anything we might expect to find in Hobbes, there is nothing in it which conflicts with Hobbes's psychology, which in fact, identifies differences between men as differences in their preponderant passions and can accommodate the man in whom pride occupies a greater place than fear.

Indeed, it is a character which actually appears in Hobbes's writings, and is, moreover, recognized there as just character. "That which gives to human actions the relish of justice," he says, "is a certain Nobleness or Gallantness of courage (rarely found), by which a man scorns to be beholden for the contentment of life, to fraud or breach of promise. This justice of Manners, is that which is meant, where justice is called a virtue."[106] He recognized that a man may keep his word, not merely because he fears the consequences of breaking it, but from "a glory or pride in appearing not to need to break it."[107] He identified magnanimity

---

106. *L.,* p. 114.
107. *L.,* pp. 108; cf. 229.

with just conduct that springs from "contempt" of injustice, and recognized that men are sometimes prepared to lose their lives rather than suffer some sorts of shame.[108] And the only hindrance to our recognizing this as a genuinely Hobbesian character is the general assertion that Hobbes always used the word "pride" in a derogatory sense.[109]

But this assertion is, in fact, too sweeping. It is, of course, true that Hobbes sometimes used the word "pride" in a derogatory sense to indicate one of the three passions preeminent in causing strife;[110] but he also identified it with generosity, courage, nobleness, magnanimity, and an endeavour for glory,[111] and he distinguished it from "vainglory," which is always a vice because it entails illusion and strife without the possibility of felicity.[112] In short, Hobbes (who took the conception "pride" from the Augustinian tradition of moral and political theology) recognized the twofold meaning which the word has always carried. Pride, in that tradition, was the passion to be Godlike. But it was recognized that this may be either the endeavour to put oneself in the place of God, or the endeavour to imitate God. The first is a delusive insolence in which a Satanic self-love, believing itself to be omnipotent, is not only the last analysis of every passion but the only operative motive, and conduct becomes the imposition of oneself upon the world of men and of things. This Hobbes, like every other moralist, recognized as a vice and an absolute bar to a peaceful condition of human circumstance: it is the pride which provokes a destroying nemesis, the pride which Heraclitus said should be put out even more than a fire. But, as Duns Scotus said, there is no vice but it is the shadow of a virtue; and in the second manner of being Godlike, self-love appears as self-knowledge and self-respect, the delusion of power over oth-

108. *E.W.*, II, 38.
109. Strauss, p. 25.
110. *L.*, pp. 57, 128, 246.
111. *L.*, p. 96.
112. *L.*, pp. 44, 77.

ers is replaced by the reality of self-control, and the glory of the invulnerability which comes from courage generates magnanimity, peace. This is the *virtue* of pride whose lineage is to be traced back to the nymph Hybris, the reputed mother of Pan by Zeus; the pride which is reflected in the *megalopsychos* of Aristotle and at a lower level in the wise man of the Stoics; the *sancta superbia* which had its place in medieval moral theology; and which was recognized by Hobbes as an alternative manner to that suggested by fear and reason of preserving one's own nature and emancipating oneself from the fear of shameful death and from the strife which this fear generates.

Nor is this idiom of the character of the just man without its counterpart in the writings of other moralists of the same general disposition as Hobbes. Spinoza, considering the same problem as Hobbes, indicated two alternative escapes into peace from the competitive propensities of human nature; the one generated by fear and prudential foresight which results in the law and order of the *civitas,* and the other the escape offered by the power of the mind over the circumstances of human life. And Hume, taking pride and humility (which, like Hobbes, he identified with fear)[113] as the simple passions, equally self-centred, recognized both as generators of virtue, but "self-esteem" as the generator of the "shining virtues"—courage, intrepidity, magnanimity, and the endeavour for the sort of glory in which "death loses its terrors" and human life its contentiousness. But whereas Hume found the merit of pride as the motive for just conduct not only in its "agreeableness" (identifying it with pleasure and humility with frustration) but also in its superior "utility,"[114] the question we have to ask ourselves about Hobbes is, Why did he not pursue this line of argument further? Why did he deny utility to pride and conclude that, in the end, "the passion to be reckoned with is fear"?

113. *Elements,* I, ix, 2.
114. *Treatise,* II, i and iii; *Enquiries,* § 263; *Essays,* xvi; The Stoic.

And to this question Hobbes himself provided a clear answer, an answer less fully elaborated than Spinoza's but in principle the same: it is not because pride does not provide an adequate motive for a successful endeavour for peace, but because of the dearth of noble characters. "This," he says, "is a generosity too rarely to be found to be presumed, especially in pursuers of wealth, command, and sensual pleasure; which are the greatest part of Mankind."[115] In short, Hobbes perceived that men lack passion rather than reason, and lack, above all, *this* passion. But where it is present, it is to be recognized as capable of generating an endeavour for peace more firmly based than any other and therefore (even in the *civitas*, where it is safe to be just) the surest motive for just conduct. Indeed, it seems almost to have been Hobbes's view that men of this character are a necessary cause of the *civitas;* and certainly it is only they who, having an adequate motive for doing so, may be depended upon to defend it when dissension deprives the sovereign of his power. And he saw in Sidney Godolphin the emblem of this character.[116] Nevertheless, even here Hobbes displays his disposition to be more interested in the causes or motives of just conduct than in the reasons for believing that we have an obligation to endeavour peace: "pride" does not supply a reason, it is only a possible alternative cause.

There is, perhaps, one further observation to be made. Fear of shameful death, provoking reason to suggest the convenient articles of peace and the manner in which they may become the pattern of human life, generates the morality of the tame man, the man who has settled for safety and has no need of nobility, generosity, magnanimity, or an endeavour for glory in order to move him to behave justly. And, insofar as this was Hobbes's view, he has been recognized as the philosopher of a so-called "bourgeois" morality. But this is an idiom of the moral life which,

---

115. *L.*, p. 108.
116. *L.*, Dedication, p. 548; *Vita* (1681), p. 240.

in spite of Hobbes's individualistic reading of human nature, seems to intimate and point towards the notion of a "common good." It seems to suggest a single approved condition of human circumstances for all conditions of men, and morality as the art in which this condition is achieved and maintained. But there are qualifications to be noticed which tend to confirm the view that, with Kant and others, he was preeminently a philosopher of the morality of individuality. First, Hobbes was primarily concerned with motives for obeying civil law; he is less concerned with what a man might otherwise do with his life than with the minimum conditions in which the endeavour for peace could be the pattern of conduct for even the least well-disposed man. These minimum conditions are that there shall be one *law* for the lion and the ox and that both should have known and adequate motives for obeying it. And this, while perhaps intimating the disposition which generated the morality of the "common good," does not itself entail it: one law does not entail one purpose. And secondly, Hobbes had this other mood, in which pride and self-esteem are recognized to supply an adequate motive for endeavouring peace, and in this mood he was unmistakably a philosopher of the morality of individuality. This idiom of morality is "aristocratic"; and it is neither inappropriate nor unexpected to find it reflected in the writings of one who (though he felt constrained to write for those whose chief desire was to "prosper") himself understood human beings as creatures more properly concerned with honour than with either survival or prosperity.

Appendix

The precise manner in which Hobbes believed a *civitas* may be "caused," or may be imagined to emerge, lies to one side of the subject of this essay, but it is an interesting topic, attractive if for no other reason than because of its difficulty, and I propose to consider it briefly.[117]

Hobbes's position is that unless something is done to change his natural condition, no man is secure against the natural "covetousness, lust, anger, and the like" of his fellows and (consequently) has nothing better to look forward to than a nasty and brutish existence, frustrated and full of contention. Even in this state of nature, men (it is true) are capable of making contracts, agreements, covenants, etc., with one another, but these, so far from substantially modifying the condition of insecurity, are themselves infected with this insecurity. And this is specially the case with covenants of mutual trust. For in these, one of the covenanters must perform his part of the bargain first, but he who does so risks being bilked; indeed, the risk that he whose part it is to be the second performer will not keep his promise (not necessarily because it may be against his interest to do so, but because "avarice" and "ambition" are apt to triumph over reason) must always be great enough to make it unreasonable for any man to consent to be a first performer. Thus, while in these conditions contracts may be made and executed, and even covenants of mutual trust, they always entail a risk which no reasonable man will take and they offer no extensive or reliable modification of the war of all men against all men.

This situation, however, would be transformed if there were a "common power" acknowledged by all men to have the authority to compel the keeping of covenants; and Hobbes's question is: How may such a "common power" be imagined to be "caused" and what must be its character?

The only manner in which such a "common power" may be erected, he tells us, is for every man to covenant with every man to transfer his natural *right* to govern himself and to preserve his

117. In the following account I have had the advantage of suggestions kindly offered me by Mr. J. M. Brown, who nevertheless must not be held responsible for the blunders it may still contain.

own nature, and to relinquish his natural *power* (such as it is) to secure the fulfilment of his own desires, to one man or an assembly of men, and to "acknowledge himself to be the author of whatsoever he that so beareth their person, shall act, or cause to be acted, in those things which concern the common peace and safety; and therein to submit their wills, every one to his will, and their judgments, to his judgment."

Now, accepting for the moment the conclusion, namely, that those who have put themselves in this situation will enjoy what they seek to enjoy, peace, what we have to consider is the intelligibility of the process by which it is reached. Certain difficulties appear. The covenant by means of which this common power is purported to be established is unmistakably what Hobbes calls a covenant of mutual trust, and it is made by men in a state of nature, consequently (unless we are given some cogent reason for thinking otherwise) it cannot be supposed to be exempt from the considerations which make all such covenants unreasonably risky undertakings for the first performer and therefore not to be relied upon by reasonable men. It is true that its terms are different from the terms of any other covenant of mutual trust; but how can its terms (that is, *what* is promised) transform a covenant of a kind in which it is unreasonably risky to be the first performer into one in which the risk (if any) is not unreasonable? It is true, also, that it is (what not all other covenants of mutual trust are) a covenant to which many are parties; but, since there is no reason why an ordinary covenant of mutual trust should not be of this sort, and if it were so, there is no reason why it should be less reasonable to suspect nonperformance on the part of at least some of the participants, the multilateral character of this covenant does not appear to distinguish it to any advantage. And further, Hobbes's words often seem to suggest that the mere entering into this covenant, the mere "signing" of it (so to speak), generates the "common power," and it is not easy to understand how this can be so.

But if we go again to what Hobbes wrote we may, perhaps,
find him to be saying something that avoids these difficulties.
This would, I think, be so if we were to interpret him as follows:
There will be "peace" and a condition in which covenants will
be lasting and constant, only if there is a Sovereign to enforce
peace and to compel the keeping of covenants. This Sovereign,
in order to perform his office, must have *authority* (that is,
right), and he must have *power*. The only way in which he can
be imagined to acquire authority is by means of a covenant of
the sort already described, and in order to have authority nothing more than this covenant is needed. Therefore such a covenant (or something like it) may be recognized as a necessary
"cause" of a *civitas*. And, further, it may, perhaps, also be recognized as empirically necessary as a means of generating the
power required by the Sovereign, because it is hardly to be imagined that a number of individuals will in fact acknowledge his
authority in the acts and dispositions of obedience which constitute his power unless they have covenanted to do so. Nevertheless, the covenant by itself is not the sufficient cause of a *civitas;*
it gives authority, but it merely promises power. The necessary
and sufficient cause of a Sovereign possessed of the authority
and the power required to establish a condition of "peace" is a
covenant of this sort combined with a sufficiently widespread
disposition (displayed in overt acts) to observe its terms; for the
Sovereign's power is only the counterpart of his subjects' disposition to obey. And consequently, we are provoked to look in
Hobbes's account for some argument which will convince us that
it is reasonable to expect that this covenant, unlike others made
in the state of nature, will be kept. For, perhaps with some colour
of paradox, it now appears that the power necessary to establish
peace and to compel the keeping of covenants is generated not
by making the covenant but only in the process of keeping it,
that is, in dispositions and acts of obedience. In short, we have
been convinced that it must always be unreasonable to be the
first performer in an ordinary covenant of mutual trust in the

state of nature, and what Hobbes has now to demonstrate to us is that it is not unreasonable for any man to be the first performer in *this* covenant of mutual trust. And it may be observed, at once, that this condition of affairs cannot be made to spring from there being a power to compel those who are to be the second performers to keep their promises, because what we are seeking is an intelligible explanation of how such a power can be "erected."

Now, on this question Hobbes seems to have made his position doubly secure. He undertakes to show us: first, that it is reasonable to be the first performer in this covenant even if there is no reasonable expectation that the other covenanters will keep their promises; and further, that there is in fact a reasonable expectation that a significant number of covenanters will keep their promises, and that in the case of *this* covenant (unlike that of ordinary covenants) this is enough to make it not unreasonable to be a first performer.

First, a party to this covenant is, to be sure, taking some risk if he obeys a Sovereign authority who is unable to compel the obedience of the other parties and if he has no reasonable expectation that they also will obey. Nevertheless, it is not an unreasonable risk because what he stands to lose is insignificant compared with what he stands to gain, and because, in fact, unless someone is the first performer in this covenant the "common power" necessary to peace can never come into existence.[118] This is a cogent argument; it observes a relevant distinction between the covenant to authorize the exercise of sovereign authority and other covenants of mutual trust, and it points out the entailment of this in respect of the reasonableness of being a first performer in this covenant; but most readers of Hobbes will look for something to fortify it. And, at least without going against anything he wrote, this may be found in the following considerations.

One of the important differences between the covenant to ac-

---

118. Perhaps, for the generation of the *civitas*, it is necessary to assume a man, not "reasonable," but proudly careless of the consequences of being the first for peace; if so, there is some authority in Hobbes for this assumption.

knowledge the authority of a Sovereign and thus endow him with power and any other covenant of mutual trust is that it may be effectively fulfilled even if all the parties do *not* behave as they have promised to behave. In an ordinary covenant of mutual trust between two the first performer is not requited unless the other keeps his word when his time comes. And this is true, also, in an ordinary covenant of mutual trust (one concerned with goods and services) in which there are many participants; the first performer, and each other performer, is deprived of something significant unless *all* the participants perform. But in this covenant among many to obey a Sovereign authority, the first performer, and each other willing performer, loses nothing if, instead of all performing, only some do so—as long as those who do are sufficient in number to generate the power necessary to compel those who are not disposed to obey. And while it may be unreasonable to expect that ambition and avarice will distract none of the parties to this covenant from keeping their promise to obey, it is not unreasonable to expect that a sufficient number will be immune from this distraction. Thus, there is a feature in this covenant which distinguishes it from all others and makes it not unreasonable to be a first performer; and every party to it is potentially a first performer. But, since what is sought by all reasonable men and what is counted upon by a first performer in this covenant is a durable condition of peace, the position is, perhaps, better understood as one in which it is not unreasonable to be a first performer and to go on performing because it is not unreasonable to expect that enough of the other parties will themselves voluntarily perform for enough of the time to generate enough power in the sovereign to force those who on any particular occasion may not be disposed to obey. For, the reasonableness of being a first performer does not depend upon his having a reasonable expectation that there will be a permanent body of particular persons who will always be disposed to requite his trust in them; it will suffice if he has a reasonable expectation that at any particular time there will be enough who are so disposed. The clouds of avarice, ambition, and the like sweep over the sky and their shadows fall now upon this man and now upon that; no single man can be depended upon to keep the covenant all the time and upon every occasion. But this is not necessary; it is enough if enough may on any occasion be reasonably depended upon to endow by their willing obedience the sovereign with enough power to terrify into obedience those who on that occasion are not disposed to obey.

The argument, then, seems to run, briefly, as follows: Natural reason warns us against being the first performer in all ordinary covenants of mutual trust; and it tells us, also, that it is in our interest to seek peace and it suggests the manner in which peace may emerge. The necessary condition of peace is a Sovereign at once authoritative and powerful. The authority of this Sovereign can derive only from a covenant of mutual trust of every man with every man in which they transfer to him their natural right to govern themselves and in which they own and acknowledge all his commands in respect of those things which concern the common peace and safety as if they were their own. But the power of this Sovereign to enforce his commands derives only from those who have thus covenanted to obey actually obeying. A start must be made somewhere, and it must be shown to be a reasonable beginning. Is it not reasonable to expect that, having been reasonable enough to have made the covenant, enough men at any one time will be reasonable enough (that is, will be free enough from avarice and ambition and the like to recognize where their interest lies) to be disposed to keep it? And if this is so, it becomes a not unreasonable risk for any man to be the first performer. And every party to this covenant is a potential first performer. "This is the generation of that great Leviathan . . . to which we owe under the Immortal God, our peace and defence."

It must be acknowledged, however, that this account shows not that it is undeniably reasonable to be a first performer in this covenant to set up a sovereign authority (or even that it is undeniably not unreasonable to be such), but only that the risk entailed here is far more reasonable (or far less unreasonable) than the risk entailed in an ordinary covenant of mutual trust. And since, as I understand it, what Hobbes is seeking is a demonstration of reasonableness and not merely the probability of superior reasonableness, I must suspect that this account is either faulty or incomplete. To what extent the supposition of a man (such as Hobbes understood Sidney Godolphin to have been) careless of the consequences of being bilked as the first performer in this covenant, a man of "pride" and not of "reason," supplies what is lacking, the reader must decide for himself.

1960

Dr. Leo Strauss on Hobbes

The renewed attention which, in recent years, the writings of Thomas Hobbes have received is noteworthy, in the first place, because it is not to be attributed to the present state of political arrangements of Western Europe, but to a fresh and scholarly interest in the writings of a man whose political philosophy is independent of and infinitely more important than his political opinions: this reexamination of Hobbes is the work, not of politicians in search of a creed or publicists in search of an excuse, but of historians and philosophers. And secondly, it is noteworthy because it has already laid the foundation for a reinterpretation of those writings which shows incomparably profounder insight and greater knowledge than went to the construction of the hitherto accepted interpretation. To a generation which did not find foolish the opinion of Vaughan that "so far as the vital development of political thought is concerned, the *Leviathan* remained, and deserved to remain, without influence and without fruit; a fantastic hybrid, incapable of propagating its kind," the announcement of "the epoch-making significance of Hobbes's political philosophy," the judgement that upon Hobbes's break with tradition "all later moral and political thought is expressly or tacitly based," the view (in short) that Hobbes was not grossly in error when he said that "civil philosophy is no older than my own book, *De Cive,*" may at first be shocking. But this certainly is the direction in which the recent studies of Hobbes's work is leading us. And even if some modification of this revolutionary conclusion should, in the end, be necessary, those who are responsible for suggesting it have at least broken down a thoroughly misleading tradition and have already given us the materials and the opportunity for a far more intelligent valuation of Hobbes's writings than was hitherto possible. There remains much to be done; but the achievement already is great.

This reinterpretation of Hobbes's philosophy is not, of course, the preserve of a single writer; many have had a hand in it. But it is safe to say that the work of Dr. Leo Strauss is of the first importance. In 1932, a paper entitled "Quelques Remarques sur la Science Politique de Hobbes," which appeared in *Recherches Philosophiques*, where among much else that is informative and suggestive he makes clear Hobbes's true place in the history of liberalism, was his first contribution. But his recently published book on the basis and genesis of Hobbes's political philosphy[1] shows him to be a leader in this work whom we may follow with profit and with confidence, if also (as we must follow all leaders in those matters) with some caution. I propose in this essay to examine his book, not with all the thoroughness it merits, but with some care, because I regard it as the most original book on Hobbes which has appeared for many years. And before going further, in case what I shall have to say might be taken to indicate a different view, I must express at once my admiration for the book as a whole, for the careful scholarship which has gone to make it, for the great subtlety of its argument, and for the brilliance of its exposition. It has the rare quality of presenting an original thesis and supporting it with an apparently conclusive argument, and at the same time of provoking thought and criticism; and even in those parts where it appears more ingenious than sound, its ingenuity is stimulating and never misleading.

1. *The Political Philosophy of Hobbes; Its Basis and Genesis*, by Leo Strauss. Translated from the German manuscript by Elsa M. Sinclair, M.A., Ph.D., Oxford, 1936.

For one who has so much that is new to propound, Dr. Strauss retains an admirable sense of proportion, only occasionally appearing to press more than is reasonable out of his material in order to prove his thesis or to give undue weight to his favourite conjectures. If the book has a fault, it lies in the very conclusiveness of the case it presents. The author occasionally protests a trifle too much, but this springs simply from the enthusiasm and conviction with which he writes. But, in general, nothing could exceed the care and conscientiousness with which the argument is pursued; and it could hardly have been made shorter than it is. It should be remarked, also, that Dr. Strauss has been exceptionally fortunate in his translator.

In dealing with this book it is not necessary to consider the question (which many commentators on philosophical texts would do well to consider), what may usefully and relevantly be said about a philosophical text? because Dr. Strauss's taste in the matter is faultless. His argument is admirably compact, complex though it is; and never for one moment is he guilty of wandering from the matter in hand to instruct us on some point irrelevant to his thesis. And we are spared that tedious and boring review of all that has previously been thought and said with which so many writers seem to think it necessary to preface their contributions. This book is written for those who already know something about Hobbes, for those who are acquainted with his writings; it is as remote as can be from those handbooks which are offered as a substitute for a first-hand study of their subject.

The task that Dr. Strauss has set himself is to defend three major theses and one minor. So far as I understand him he wishes to establish:

(i) That Hobbes's political philosophy shows a complete break with "tradition" (i.e., Aristotle, Scholasticism, Natural Law), not so much because of its scientific character, but because of the "moral attitude" that it embodies.

(ii) That the real and the original foundation of Hobbes's polit-

ical philosophy is a "new moral attitude." The "scientific" method
of argument which Hobbes used in all the later expositions of that
philosophy is a later addition, obscuring the real foundation, and
is, in fact, if not inconsistent with it, at least unnecessary to it.
Hobbes's political philosophy (unlike Spinoza's) is not a naturalistic philosophy.

(iii) That Hobbes's philosophical development may be divided
into three periods which are not merely periods of his life, but
successive steps in his search for an adequate political philosophy:

(a) Early education: Aristotle; Scholasticism; Oxford.

(b) "Humanistic" period (1608 to 1630 *circa*): characterized
by an interest in literature, a study of history (particularly Thucydides), and a temporary acceptance of the "traditional
norms" of a political philosophy.

(c) Later philosophical period (1630–79), which begins with
his "discovery of Euclid's *Elements*," and is characterized by the
construction of his system of philosophy under the influence of
a "new moral attitude" and the method of modern science: Euclid and Galileo.

(iv) That all later moral and political thought is based expressly
or tacitly upon the break with "tradition" which Hobbes achieved;
it replaces natural law by natural right as the starting point of a
philosophical explanation of civil institutions, and issues in a theory of sovereignty characteristic of all modern (as distinct from
Ancient and Medieval) political theory.

It will be seen at once that part of what Dr. Strauss wishes to
establish breaks really new ground, while part is to some extent
familiar, although perhaps it has never before been argued for
with such confidence. And it will be seen also that these theses
are connected with one another closely enough for it to be impossible for either Dr. Strauss or his critics to deal with them
separately. They do not exactly stand or fall together, but they
hang together in Dr. Strauss's mind as a single whole and they
can profitably be considered only in that way. Nevertheless some
opportunity is offered for analysis, and for the approval or accep-

tance of some parts of his work more readily than others. Let us
first of all be clear about what Dr. Strauss wishes to prove, because it is a complicated set of theses which cannot with justice
be stated shortly. And when we have before us clearly what is to
be maintained about the writings of Hobbes, we can go on to
consider the evidence and the arguments adduced.

"As G. C. Robertson observed in his *Hobbes,* fifty years ago,
'the whole of (Hobbes's) political doctrine . . . doubtless had its
main lines fixed when he was still a mere observer of men and
manners, and not yet a mechanical philosopher' (p. 57). It is,
therefore, only natural to attempt a coherent exposition of
Hobbes's 'pre-scientific' thought on 'men and manners', of his
original view, not yet distorted by scientific 'explanations', of human life" (p. xiii). Dr. Strauss, then, wishes to maintain that there
is to be found in the early writings of Hobbes evidence that his
political philosophy, later to be elaborated under the influence
of Euclid and Galileo, has its *genesis* in a "prescientific" and informal observation of the behaviour of men, an observation
which, as he explains it, resulted in a "moral attitude." "The experience, underlying Hobbes's view of human life, must be
traced back to a specific moral attitude which compels its holder
to experience and see man in Hobbes's particular way" (p. xiv).
This "moral attitude" is "Hobbes's original view" and it is "independent both of tradition and modern science": it was present
in his mind before he became acquainted with "modern science," and it is in conflict with the moral attitude or set of norms
provided by traditional moral and political philosophy. When Dr.
Strauss comes to explain this moral attitude in detail he describes it as a "new moral attitude," and, if I understand him
correctly, it is new in two senses—it is new because it is "untradi-
tional," because it is a break with the Aristotelian tradition, and
it is new because it appears in Hobbes's writings as a successor
to an original acceptance of the old or traditional moral attitude;
that is, it is new in the history of moral philosophy and (at a certain point) it is new in the history of Hobbes's own intellectual

development. As Dr. Strauss sees the situation, then, Hobbes's first and original attack upon the problems of political philosophy was made "on the basis of a study of the passions." "From the outset he sought to answer the question of the best form of State with regard not to man's essential being and the place occupied by him in the universe, but to experience of human life, to application, and therefore with particular reference to the passions" (p. 110). And the way of thinking pursued by Hobbes in this original attempt is described as "the method of the *Rhetoric*," because the dominating methodological influence upon him at the time was the method Aristotle followed in the *Rhetoric*. In the earliest period of all Hobbes came very much under the influence of the particular theory of the passions expounded by Aristotle in his *Rhetoric,* and that influence is to some extent still evident in his later writings; but long after it had lost its full force, the influence of the "method of the *Rhetoric*" remained. And I say Hobbes's "way of thinking" because there remains little or nothing which Hobbes actually wrote on this plan, nor can we suppose that he wrote anything on this plan which has subsequently been lost. The "method of the *Rhetoric*," then, is contrasted by Dr. Strauss with the method of thought and writing which Hobbes subsequently adopted under the influence of his "preoccupation with exact science"; it is contrasted with "Euclid," with "modern science," and with the "resolutive-compositive method" which, it is said, Hobbes acquired from Galileo.

Now, the conclusion towards which Dr. Strauss is leading us is that because we have hitherto paid attention only to those of Hobbes's writings which come after his "discovery of Euclid's *Elements*" and are conceived in the terms of a mechanical-scientific view of nature, we have been misled into thinking that Hobbes's political philosophy is (like Spinoza's) a naturalistic philosophy; whereas the truth is that this political philosophy was conceived before ever Hobbes became a "mechanical philosopher" and is conceived in terms, not of nature, but of a "moral

down to elaborate the doctrines which appeared later in *De Corpore* and *De Homine,* and to the account of his intellectual activities which Hobbes gives in his Autobiography and in some of his Prefaces. This evidence is not, of course, conclusive; the inference that because *De Cive* was composed before *De Corpore* or *De Homine* its doctrines are necessarily independent of the doctrines of the later works has frequently been made by interpreters of Hobbes, but there is not much to be said in its favour, and if no other evidence were available it could not be counted conclusive. The argument from "biographical priority" is the weakest of all arguments, and cannot even take an independent place in a catena of evidence. Setting aside this ambiguous biographical evidence, we are asked to consider the writings of Hobbes which were actually composed before the crucial period in his life, 1629–34, when he became acquainted with Euclid's *Elements* and Galileo and occupied himself with "scientific" studies. What is suggested is that in those early writings is to be found, undistorted by "science," the original foundation of Hobbes's politics. But a difficulty at once arises, a difficulty of which, of course, Dr. Strauss is aware, but which he nowhere candidly admits. The fact is that there exists *no* ordered account of Hobbes's political theory before 1640. In other words, all the evidence that might be conclusive is contaminated by "science." For what are these "prescientific" works? They are (i) the Introduction to the translation of Thucydides (about 1628), (ii) A Short Tract on First Principles (about 1630), and Dr. Strauss adds a third, though he dates it 1635 and so makes it fall outside the relevant period, (iii) the two English digests of Aristotle's *Rhetoric.* In short, the materials are, as Dr. Strauss admits, "very sparse"; the only certainly uncontaminated work which deals in any way with political philosophy is the Introduction to Thucydides, and Dr. Strauss is obliged to build upon this to a considerable extent. He believes that the translation represents a fundamentally important step in the construction of Hobbes's political philosophy; and with enthusiasm he extracts all, and perhaps more than all, that can be got from the Introduction. But there is a third line of approach, a third place where we may look for evidence. If we can find in Hobbes's later writings on political philosophy, in the *Elements of Law* (1640), *De Cive* (1642), and *Leviathan* (1651) evidence of a view of things which is independent of the "scientific" form of these writings, or if we could find evidence in these contaminated writings of a gradual move towards a more and more "mechanical" theory, we might conclude that the prescientific view was an earlier or an original view, or argue that the increasingly "scientific" character of these writings suggests an earlier period in which Hobbes's mind was even less influenced by his scientific theories than it appears to have been even in the earliest of these writings, the *Elements of Law*. And further, if these writings contain inconsistencies which could easily be resolved, or at least explained, by supposing that the "science" in them was merely superimposed upon a theory the real basis of which was independent of "science," we might take this as genuine evidence for the existence of a nonscientific, original view, never completely abandoned.

This third line of approach seems to me the most promising, and indeed it is I think taken to be the most promising by Dr. Strauss, who is frequently to be found quoting the later "scientific" writings to support the thesis that an earlier "nonscientific" theory existed and is fundamental to Hobbes's political philosophy. In fact, sometimes it seems as if he scarcely distinguishes between the second and the third line of argument, he passes from one to the other so freely. But promising as this line of argument is, it is, nevertheless, dangerous, and calls for the greatest care in handling. That Dr. Strauss makes the most of it, goes without saying; but that this most is entirely satisfactory seems to me doubtful; and it is at least disconcerting to find these later writings so freely appealed to in the attempt to elucidate a view of things which, *ex hypothesi*, is prior to them and in conflict with their character. It is, really, one thing to prove (as Dr. Strauss proves) that there is marked change and development towards a more and more "scientific" theory in the *Elements of Law, De Cive,* and *Leviathan,* but it is quite another to infer from this development the existence of an "original" theory altogether "nonscientific," and it is another still to infer that this "original" theory was never really abandoned. It is indeed certain that, in his latest writings, Hobbes did abandon it—Dr. Strauss himself admits as much; and it is a lapse from the scrupulous attention that Dr. Strauss usually pays to the smallest movement in Hobbes's intellectual history to suppose that this abandonment was unintentional and not the real Hobbes. As Dr. Strauss shows, Hobbes did, on more than one occasion, entirely reject views which at one time he held as pertinaciously as he ever held any views. For example, the whole period of his life in which he "turned to history" for the material for his political philosophy Hobbes later considered to have been misguided; and the view expressed in all his later writings of the essential wrongness of all opinion as such must lead us to conclude that, as far as Hobbes himself was concerned, a political philosophy based upon a moral opinion or "attitude" was insecurely based. Somehow this merely moral basis had to be transformed, and Hobbes accomplished the transformation.

These, however, are points of detail; and while they bear upon the thesis that Hobbes's "original" view is also (in spite of appearances) his mature and considered view, they do not touch the thesis that an original "nonscientific" view existed, prior to and independent of Hobbes's later writings. Here the chief handicap is, I think, the unsatisfactory character of the evidence. But Dr. Strauss's argument fails to carry conviction, not from any failure to deal as faithfully as may be with the available evidence, but from what I should consider his unduly narrow and too precise separation of "science" from "nonscience" in Hobbes's writings. "Hobbes was over forty when he 'discovered' Euclid's *Elements,* and not until after that did he begin to take a serious interest in natural science" (p. 29). For Dr. Strauss, then, "science" came into Hobbes's life with the "discovery" of Euclid's *Elements* and the influence of Galileo; and it gave him a "method," a "form of proof" and nothing more. But as I see the matter, Hobbes was never a scientist in any true sense, that is, his "science" is really conceived throughout as an epistemology. He is never concerned with the scientific observation of the natural world, but always with what the character of the world must be if we are to have any knowledge of it; he is not concerned with the natural world for its own sake, but with the causes of sensation. Not merely do his politics start from "human nature," the passions, but his whole view of the natural world also. So far from this interest in the natural world appearing suddenly in his life about 1630, it was an interest which he was never without and which he indulged when it became necessary for his theory. And even when the influence of Galileo was at its height, Hobbes never moderates his contempt for "experimental science" and his considered view that from observation no universal truths can be inferred. And Part I of the *Elements of Law*, for example, does not indicate an entirely new (for Hobbes) approach to political philosophy, but merely a more determined attempt to work out a satisfactory theory of human nature and the passions than he had previously achieved; it is the "method of the *Rhetoric*" not abandoned, but extended. It is impossible, however, to discuss here all that "science" means for Hobbes; it must be enough to say that I do not think that Dr. Strauss in identifying "science" in Hobbes with "the method of Galileo" really does justice to his subject. I think, then, that he has proved his case that at some early period Hobbes did conceive his political philosophy in terms of a moral fear of violent death and an immoral vanity or pride—although there is no work in existence in which such a theory is expounded fully without the contamination of "science." But I think that he is wrong in supposing either that his early theory was conceived entirely in moral terms,[2] or that the

2. That "vanity" "must of necessity be treated from the moral standpoint" (p. 169) is, I should have thought, doubtful. Hobbes's own treatment of it in terms of "illusion" surely takes it out of the purely moral sphere. Cf. Strauss, pp. 19, 27. And

replacement of "vanity" by "the striving for power" (that is, by a "neutral" term) was not a real advance in Hobbes's theory and conceived as such by him. Hobbes's theory may not be of the *simple* "naturalistic" character that it has often been supposed to be, but neither is it of the *simple* "moral" character Dr. Strauss suggests. It is "naturalistic" not in contrast to "moral," but in an attempt to find a firmer basis than merely a moral opinion. And if this is so, Dr. Strauss's view that "the most mature presentation of [Hobbes's] philosophy, that is the *Leviathan,* is by no means an adequate source for an understanding of Hobbes's moral and political ideas" (p. 170), can be accepted in only a qualified form. But the really valuable contributions which Dr. Strauss has to make are the demonstration that Hobbes had and retained a view by which just and unjust actions could be distinguished independently of human legislation, and that Hobbes's political philosophy is not of the simple naturalistic type that it has so frequently been taken to be.

Dr. Strauss's view of the relation of Hobbes's political philosophy to "tradition" is in the main satisfactorily maintained. But here again, there is a certain amount of ambiguity owing to the comparatively narrow conception of tradition with which he works. "Tradition" means, in this book, "the classical and theological tradition," it means Aristotle and Scholasticism, and it means in particular the "moral attitude," the set of norms with which this classical and theological tradition worked. That Hobbes shows a complete, though gradual, break with these norms, and (in this sense) this tradition, is proved too conclusively to be denied. The view that "fear of violent death" is the one passion or sentiment in man which is moral and the root of all moral behaviour is certainly something new and revolutionary; though in a different and less systematic way a similar rejection of both the form and the content of the classical and theo-

---

the so-called "selfishness" of man was not, for Hobbes, a moral doctrine, but an epistemological doctrine.

logical tradition is to be found, for example, in the *Discorsi* of
Machiavelli. But the view that "pride" or "vanity" is the passion
against which all the force of civil society is expressly directed
has its place in the medieval tradition: and I do not think due
weight is given in this account of the genesis of Hobbes's view to
what he may have learnt from his early instruction in this Stoic-
Christian tradition, as distinct from what he learnt from Aristotle's theory of the passions which appears in the *Rhetoric*. And
Dr. Strauss's rejection (pp. 3–5) of Dilthey's attempt to relate
Hobbes's theory of the passions to that of the Stoa, on the ground
of a difference in certain details, is neither convincing nor quite
consistent with his later (p. 150) remarks about the influence
which Plato and the Stoic theory had upon the subsequent development of Hobbes's analysis of fear and vanity. But a more
important omission is, I think, the failure to link Hobbes's political philosophy on to a different tradition in political philosophy,
the Epicurean tradition. Hobbes's writings, in many respects,
belong to that recrudescence of Epicurean philosophy which
was so important in the intellectual life of the sixteenth and early
seventeenth centuries. The biographical evidence for connect-
ing Hobbes with the neo-Epicurean movement is conclusive;
and whatever the striking differences between Hobbes's ethical
doctrines and those of Epicurus, his completely different conception of the *summum bonum* upon which Dr. Strauss remarks
(p. 134) and which had been remarked upon before by Guyau,
La Morale d'Epicure (p. 195), we ought not to allow them to
obscure the great similarity. Considering the kind of works in
which the views of Epicurus are handed down, we could not
expect connected discussions, and one at least of Hobbes's
achievements was to construct a comprehensive system where
before there were only scattered aphorisms. But to this I will
return when I discuss what I have called Dr. Strauss's fourth
thesis.

Perhaps the most ingenious and acute part of Dr. Strauss's
book is taken up with an attempt to trace the stages of the devel-

opment of Hobbes's philosophical interests. There is little I can
say about it; I find it in the main convincing. But it is important
to see just what is original in what Dr. Strauss has to say. Robertson in his book on Hobbes divided the life of his subject into
three main periods—Youth—Oxford; the Scholar; the Philosopher. And Dr. Strauss, for the most part, concurs with this division. But he has two important additions to make. In the first
place, the period which Robertson called that of "the Scholar,"
Dr. Strauss calls the "humanistic period"; and since it is the period, in his view, during which Hobbes conceived the main plan
of his philosophy insofar as it did not depend upon the later "mechanical" conception of nature, he devotes long chapters to a
close examination of the writings of Hobbes which came from it
and to a minute study of the interests which they disclose. He
admits that, in some respects, this period was a *cul de sac,* that
it led to what, when he got there, Hobbes saw was unsatisfactory;
but nevertheless, it was the great formative period of Hobbes's
life, the period in which his mind was uncontaminated either
with "modern science" or "tradition." True, during this period
Hobbes still, apparently, believed in the "traditional norms," but
his study of history and of Thucydides was itself a break with
traditional procedure. Dr. Strauss's first addition is, then, a much
more thorough examination than has ever before been undertaken of Hobbes during the years 1608 to 1630, an examination
comparable only in the study of Hobbes to that which Brandt
executed for the years 1630–55. But, in the second place, these
three periods into which the life of Hobbes is divided have for
Dr. Strauss not the mere biographical significance that they had
for Robertson, but a philosophical significance. Hobbes, for Dr.
Strauss, is not a mere wanderer from one interest to another;
he is from the first a philosopher whose changes of interest are
purposeful and full of significance for his philosophy itself. From
philosophy Hobbes turns to history and literature, and from history and literature he "returns to philosophy." And since for a
philosopher to desert philosophy is strange and disconcerting,

Dr. Strauss has set himself to find out the reason for this aberrance—has set himself to show that it is not really an aberrance
at all but part of a planned campaign. And the Introduction to
and the translation of Thucydides gives him his material. "Philosophy," we are told, gave Hobbes "the rational precepts for the
right behaviour of man," and up to this point Hobbes did not
radically question what he had got. What however was presented
to him was the problem of how to make rational precept effective, the application of the precepts. His turn from philosophy
to history was his attempt to meet this problem. And Dr. Strauss
shows how in this Hobbes was following and creating a tradition
in thought which belonged to his time. But the end of the adven-
ture was unexpected—Hobbes found in history what he was
looking for, but he found also in himself a new scepticism about
the rational precepts themselves, and this scepticism was the
starting point of the third period of his intellectual activity, a period alas marred by the intrusion also of "modern science." The
view is worked out most effectively in Dr. Strauss's enthusiastic
pages; and my admiration for the whole argument is only qualified by the feeling that it gives to Hobbes's activity an over-
systematic character, that it makes Hobbes not a figure in that
period of restless, sometimes distracted, curiosity and activity to
which he belongs, but rather in a later period when a Kant or a
Hegel could and did pursue their objects with a greater discipline and a more coherent plan. And indeed, this philosopher
whose whole activity is directed by such exaggerated consistency
hardly squares with, for example, the view (p. 56) that Hobbes
was capable of momentarily adopting a strange doctrine under
the immediate influence of Descartes, or the manifold inconsistencies of even his most thoroughly executed writings.

The thesis of Dr. Strauss we have still to consider is that in
which he maintains that Hobbes's political philosophy not only
involves a break with past tradition, but contains the seed of all
later moral and political thought. The striking new departure
which he finds in Hobbes is the substitution of a natural claim

or right in place of a natural law, the substitution of will for law, as the starting point of a political philosophy. He has not much to say about this, but what he says is excellent and full of insight. Contrasted with the "classical and theological tradition," this starting point is certainly new; the pure individualistic standpoint of Hobbes's theory is certainly one respect in which he might be considered "the founder of modern political philosophy." And the modern concept of sovereignty which sprang from this new starting point involves perhaps the greatest revolution there has been in Western European political thought. But some qualification is, I think, needed before Hobbes is seen in his true place. First, the natural law theory did not die at once, even otherwise "modern" thinkers such as Locke have it embedded in their theories, and it did not die without resurrection. Indeed, it would be truer to say that it has never died at all, but has suffered transformation and a renewal of life. And secondly, although Hobbes set an example followed in one way or another by almost every later political thinker of starting with will instead of law, he never had a satisfactory or coherent theory of volition, and the whole Epicurean tradition to which he belonged did not bear fruit until this lack was remedied, and the remedy was, in fact, the union of a reconstituted natural law theory with Hobbes's Epicurean theory—a union indicated in such phrases as Rousseau's "General Will," Hegel's "Rational Will," and Bosanquet's "Real Will." The most profound movement in modern political philosophy is, as I see it, a revivification of the Stoic natural law theory achieved by the grafting upon it an Epicurean theory; it springs from the union of the two great traditions of political philosophy inherited by Western Europe from the ancient world. Its greatness is that it is a genuine theory and not a merely eclectic composition; and that it has not yet succeeded in finding an entirely satisfactory expression is certainly not a sign of its moribund condition. It is indeed something in its favour that it has maintained itself in the world for a considerable time without the advantage of that extreme type of orthodox precision which belonged to the Stoic natural law theory in its prime. Hobbes's importance is that he was the first in modern times to experiment with the cultivation of the "slip" which modern political thought has grafted on to the old natural law theory to create something more comprehensive and coherent than either: never before or since has the Epicurean tradition had so acute an exponent or received so masterly a statement. In short, I think it is an exaggeration to speak of Hobbes as "the founder of modern political philosophy." A writer so completely devoid of a satisfactory philosophy of volition lacks something vital to modern political thought. But he is certainly the founder of one of the essential elements in the political thought of the period which has followed him.

It will be seen, then, that there are various points at which I cannot follow Dr. Strauss. But that does not detract from my view that he has given us a book of the greatest interest, that he has to some extent transformed our notions about Hobbes and has said more that is true and relevant about Hobbes's political philosophy than has been said for a great number of years. And it is impossible to doubt that anyone who reads this book will look forward to its half-promised sequel, a study of the detailed character of Hobbes's mature theory, with eager anticipation.

1937

4

Leviathan: a Myth

This is a conversation piece, a flight of fancy; its theme is philosophical literature. Of all the books that have been written since the world began, by far the larger number are books whose virtue is to serve some special and limited interest. These are not works of art; they do not pretend to belong to literature in the proper sense. But now and again, by some odd misunderstanding of its character, a true masterpiece of literature gets hidden away in this vast library of fugitive and functional writings. And there it remains, lost to all except a few professional readers, who themselves (as like as not) understand it only professionally. Something of this sort has happened to the book called *Leviathan,* written in the seventeenth century by Thomas Hobbes. *Leviathan* has passed for a book of philosophy and a book about politics, and consequently it has been supposed to interest only the few who concern themselves with such things. But I believe it to be a work of art in the proper sense, one of the masterpieces of the literature of our language and civilization. What does this mean?

We are apt to think of a civilization as something solid and external, but at bottom it is a collective dream. "Insofar as the soul is in the body," says Plotinus, "it lies in deep sleep." What a people dreams in this earthly sleep is its civilization. And the substance of this dream is a myth, an imaginative interpretation of human existence, the perception (not the solution) of the mystery of human life.

The office of literature in a civilization is not to break the dream, but perpetually to recall it, to recreate it in each generation, and even to make more articulate the dream-powers of a people. We, whose participation in the dream is imperfect and largely passive, are, in a sense, its slaves. But the comparative freedom of the artist springs not from any faculty of wakefulness (not from any opposition to the dream), but from his power to dream more profoundly; his genius is to dream that he is dreaming. And it is this that distinguishes him from the scientist, whose perverse genius is to dream that he is awake. The project of science, as I understand it, is to solve the mystery, to wake us from our dream, to destroy the myth; and were this project fully achieved, not only should we find ourselves awake in a profound darkness, but a dreadful insomnia would settle upon mankind, not less intolerable for being only a nightmare.

The gift of the greatest literature—of poetry—is a gift of imagination. Its effect is an expansion of our faculty of dreaming. Under its inspiration the familiar outlines of the common dream fade, new perceptions, and emotions hitherto unfelt, are excited within us, the till-now settled fact dissolves once more into infinite possibility, and we become aware that the myth (which is the substance of the dream) has acquired a new quality, without our needing to detect the precise character of the change. But from a book of philosophy, when it reaches the level of literature (as it sometimes does), a more direct, a less subtle consequence may be expected to spring. Its gift is not an access of imaginative power, but an increase of knowledge; it will prompt and it will instruct. In it we shall be reminded of the common dream that binds the generations together, and the myth will be made more intelligible to us. And consequently, we must seek the meaning of such a book in its vision of the myth.

The myth which Hobbes inherited was the subtle and complex interpretation of human life which, springing from many sources, distinguished medieval Christian civilization. It is, moreover, the myth which no subsequent experience or reflection has succeeded in displacing from the minds of European peoples. The human race, and the world it inhabits, so runs the myth, sprang from the creative act of God, and was as perfect as its creator. But, by an original sin, mankind became separated from the source of its happiness and peace. This sin was Pride, the perverse exaltation of the creature, by which man became a god to himself. Thenceforth there lay in man's nature a hidden principle, the antagonist of his happiness. But while corrupted man pursued his blind desires, an enemy of himself and of his kind, divine grace set a limit to human self-destruction, and promised a restoration of the shattered order, an ultimate salvation. This, briefly, is the myth that gave coherence to the dream. Of the many who contributed to its construction, I suppose it owes most to the imagination of St. Paul and St. Augustine. But it was never quite fixed or finished, always there remained within it certain tensions and potentialities. And it was saved from degeneration into a formula, not merely by the theologians, but by the true custodians of the dream, the poets and the artists of the era. And it received at the very moment when Hobbes was writing *Leviathan* a fresh, if somewhat eccentric, expression in the two epics of Milton.

At first sight, it might seem that the project of *Leviathan* is nothing less than the replacement of this imaginative perception of the mystery of human life by another and altogether different myth. Man, Hobbes tells us, is a solitary creature, the inhabitant of a world which contains the materials for the satisfaction of all his desires save one—the desire to continue forever the enjoyment of an endless series of·satisfactions. He is solitary in the sense that he belongs to no order and has no obligations. His world, into which he has been carried as if in his sleep, provides all he can wish for, because his desires are centred upon no final achievement, but are confined to obtaining what he has set his mind upon in each moment of his existence. And it is not the transitoriness of his satisfaction that hinders a man's happiness, but the constant fear that death may supervene and put an end to satisfaction by terminating desire. There is indeed a lesser fear, the fear that his natural powers will be insufficient to assure him of the satisfaction of his next desire. For a man, though he is solitary, is not alone in the world, and must compete with others of his kind for the good things of life. But this lesser fear may be ignored by those who possess a certain nobility of temperament which refuses the indignity of unconditional competition, or it may be removed by coming to some agreement with his fellow inhabitants of the world, an agreement which may establish a kind of superficial peace and orderliness. But the great fear, the fear of death, is permanent and unassuaged. Life is a dream which no knowledge that mankind can acquire is able to dissipate.

The destiny of man is ruled by no Providence, and there is no place in it for perfection or even for lasting satisfaction. He is largely dependent upon his own inventiveness; but this, in spite of its imperfection, is powerful enough to create a civilized life out of the very fears and compulsions that belong to his nature and circumstance.

To those brought up in the older myth, this will appear an unduly disenchanted interpretation of the mystery of human life. But there can be no mistaking its character. It is myth, not science. It is a perception of mystery, not a pretended solution. But is it a genuine revision of the myth of our civilization, or must it be regarded as a personal eccentricity, a failure to participate in the common dream? Certainly it appeared shocking to Hobbes's contemporaries, upon whom it came with but little warning. And certainly, from time to time, there have appeared enemies of our civilization, exponents of a counterfeit myth. But I think if we look closely at *Leviathan* we may find in it the emphasis, perhaps the overemphasis, of one passage in the inherited myth, rather than the private dream of an eccentric or the malicious invention of an outcast.

Pride and sensuality, the too much and the too little—these are the poles between which, according to our dream, human life swings. The subtlety of the old myth lay in the fineness of its perception of these extremes and the imaginative power with which it filled the space between. If it erred, it was perhaps in a partiality for the too much. The myth of the Fall of Man, says Berdyaev, "is at bottom a proud idea. . . . If man fell away from God, he must have been an exalted creature, endowed with great freedom and power." But in the myth of our civilization as it appears in *Leviathan* the emphasis is on the opposite pole; it recalls man to his littleness, his imperfection, his mortality, while at the same time recognizing his importance to himself. This passage in the common dream is one that our literature since the seventeenth century has not allowed us to forget. It cannot, of course, be said that Hobbes was the first to perceive its significance. But he lived at the moment in our history when this potentiality of the traditional myth was ready to declare itself, but before the tide of science, with its project of destroying all myth, had begun to sweep over our civilization. And what makes *Leviathan* a masterpiece of philosophical literature is the profound logic of Hobbes's imagination, his power as an artist. Hobbes recalls us to our mortality with a deliberate conviction, with a subtle and sustained argument. He, with a sure and steady irony, does what Swift could do with only an intermittent brilliance, and what the literature of Existentialism is doing today with an exaggerated display of emotion and a false suggestion of novelty.

1947

Index

This book is set in 11 on 13 New Caledonia, redrawn by
John Quaranta in 1978 from William Addison Dwiggins's
typeface Caledonia, designed in 1938–39 and first used in 1941.
Caledonia has been described as hard-working and lively. Highly
legible and straightforward, it is one of the most widely used book
types of all time.

This book is printed on paper that is acid-free
and meets the requirements of the American National Standard
for Permanence of Paper for Printed Library Materials,
Z39.48-1992. ⊗

Book design by Erin Kirk New, Athens, Georgia
Typography by Graphic Composition, Inc., Athens, Georgia
Printed and bound by Sheridan Books, Inc., Ann Arbor, Michigan

Author's Note

The texts of Hobbes's works referred to are, with the exceptions of *Leviathan* and the *Elements of Law*, those published in the *English Works of Thomas Hobbes*, edited by Molesworth, 11 volumes, 1839 (referred to as *E.W.*), and in the *Opera Latina*, edited by Molesworth, 5 volumes, 1845 (referred to as *O.L.*). References to *Leviathan* (*L.*) are to the pages of the Clarendon Press reprint (1909) of the edition of 1651. References to the *Elements of Law* are to the edition by Tönnies, Cambridge, 1928.

Preface

The edition of Hobbes's *Leviathan* in the Blackwell's Political Texts was published in 1946, and it was then the only easily available edition of this work. But now that there are many others it has been allowed to go out of print. The *Introduction* I wrote for it has also been overtaken by the tide of more recent writing on the subject: the intervening years have been a notable period in Hobbes scholarship. It has, however, a certain meretricious buoyancy and I have consented to the publisher's wish that it should remain in print. I have removed some of its more obvious blemishes and I have put it with three other pieces on Hobbes. The first came out of a lecture given at the University of Nottingham and was subsequently published in *Rationalism in Politics*, the second was originally published in *Politica*, and the third was a broadcast talk. I am grateful to Mr. James Cotton for his kindness in reading the proofs.

St. Valentine's Day, 1974 M.O.

reason as merely hypothetical or instrumental and improperly invoking the older meaning of reason as sovereign master or guide. In an elaborate discussion, in which he considers the very different arguments of Strauss and Howard Warrender on this question, Oakeshott shows that Hobbes did not contradict himself in this way. Hobbes never confused rational conduct with moral conduct, and he therefore never abandoned his instrumental notion of reasoning for the sovereign reason of the classical tradition. Oakeshott concedes to Warrender that there are places in which Hobbes writes as though he did believe there were "natural laws" imposing a "natural obligation" on men to endeavor peace, but he ascribes to Hobbes in these places an exoteric intention to show his contemporaries where their duties lay and to conceal his more radical teaching.

Oakeshott considers one other objection to Hobbes's interpretation of the moral life: that Hobbes's solution to the human predicament privileges fear and the desire for security over pride and thereby one-sidedly defends the morality of the tame man, or even the bourgeois man. But Oakeshott shows that there is evidence in Hobbes's writings of an alternative derivation of the endeavor for peace out of the passion of pride. The presence of this aristocratic element in Hobbes's moral outlook refutes the simple designation of it as "bourgeois." In general, while Oakeshott is willing to concede the bourgeois character of Locke's moderate brand of liberalism, he believes that the term grossly underestimates the radical individuality that lies at the heart of Hobbes's moral outlook.

How are we to judge Oakeshott's interpretation of Hobbes? That is a question that lies beyond the scope (and charge) of this Foreword. One thing, though, can be asserted with confidence: Oakeshott has given us a Hobbes that is vastly more interesting, imaginative, complicated, and compelling than almost any other. After reading Oakeshott's essays, one wants to go back and read Hobbes.

PAUL FRANCO

tails the replacement of reason by will as the foundation of political authority. Herein lies the historic significance of Hobbes for
Oakeshott: he is the first thorough expositor of the tradition that
explores political life in terms of the master-conceptions of will
and artifice as opposed to reason and nature.

It is Hobbes's voluntarism and individualism that receive the
greatest emphasis in Oakeshott's introduction to *Leviathan*. And
Oakeshott is particularly concerned to refute the view that
Hobbes, though an individualist at the beginning of his theory,
ends up as some sort of absolutist. Hobbes's austere idea of authority is ultimately more compatible with individual liberty than
is the classical notion of reason and rule by "those who know."
"[I]t is Reason, not Authority, that is destructive of individuality."
Oakeshott puts this point in the most provocative way: "Hobbes
is not an absolutist precisely because he is an authoritarian. . . .
Indeed, Hobbes, without himself being a liberal, had in him
more of the philosophy of liberalism than most of its professed
defenders."

The most charming piece in this collection is *"Leviathan:* A
Myth," which was originally delivered as a radio talk in 1947.
Here again Oakeshott dismisses the interpretation of *Leviathan*
as a work of reductive science, considering it instead as a work
of art, a profound and imaginative exploration of the myth or
collective dream of our civilization. After tracing the Christian
roots of this myth, Oakeshott concludes that there can be no
mistaking the character of Hobbes's rendering of the human
condition in *Leviathan.* "It is myth, not science. It is perception
of mystery, not a pretended solution."

In the latest of the essays in this volume, "The Moral Life in
the Writings of Thomas Hobbes" (1960), Oakeshott returns to
the issue of the nature and role of reason in Hobbes's thought.
The question around which this essay revolves is whether the
conduct that Hobbes held to be preeminently rational, namely,
endeavoring peace, he also held to be morally obligatory, and, if
so, whether Hobbes was not thereby contradicting his view of

mology"—but because it represents Hobbes's attempt "to find a firmer basis than merely a moral opinion" for his political philosophy.

Oakeshott also qualifies Strauss's rather grand claim that Hobbes was the originator of a new tradition in political philosophy and the founder of modern political philosophy. Though Oakeshott accepts Strauss's thesis that Hobbes's political philosophy, in its substitution of right for law as the basis of the state, represents a break with the dominant natural-law tradition, he does not see this move as completely unprecedented, and he argues that Strauss neglects Hobbes's significant affinities with an earlier, Epicurean tradition. Beyond this, Oakeshott argues that Hobbes also lacks something vital to modern political thought, namely, a satisfactory theory of volition. Here Oakeshott expresses a rare criticism of Hobbes, one that reflects his own Hegelian background—he cites Hegel's doctrine of the rational will as an attempted remedy to this defect—and suggests the direction Oakeshott's own reconstitution of Hobbes's civil philosophy will take.

Almost a decade passed—a tumultuous one in world events—before Oakeshott's next writing on Hobbes appeared. This was his now-famous introduction to *Leviathan*, published in 1946. The version of the Introduction found in this volume is slightly revised from the original and bears the imprint of some of Oakeshott's later thinking on Hobbes and civil association. Many of the themes that were sketched in the essay on Strauss are here developed and gathered into a coherent and strikingly novel image of Hobbes's thought. Oakeshott sweeps away the received view of Hobbes's philosophy as naturalistic and grounded in a scientific doctrine of materialism, suggesting instead that the thread that runs through Hobbes's system is an idea of philosophy as reasoning. Hobbesian "reasoning," however, is not to be confused with the more substantial Reason of the classical tradition. It yields only hypothetical or conditional knowledge; it can never provide us with knowledge of ends. In terms of political philosophy, this skeptical doctrine of the limits of reasoning en-